STUDYING FILMS

student editions

STUDYING THE MATRIX

Anna Dawson

auteur

Anna Dawson

is a media education specialist, film journalist and Lecturer in Cinema Studies at Nottingham Trent University.

Dedication

Thanks to Dan, for all the encouragement, tea and toast.

Studying The Matrix
First published in 2003; revised 'student edition' first published in 2008 by
Auteur, The Old Surgery, 9 Pulford Road, Leighton Buzzard LU7 1AB
www.auteur.co.uk
Copyright © Auteur 2008

Series design: Nikki Hamlett
Cover image © Warner Bros. / Moviestore Collection
All stills © Warner Bros. / Moviestore Collection except page 7 (BFI Stills); pages
11, 17, 36 and 89 (Aquarius Collection)
Set by AMP Ltd, Dunstable, Bedfordshire
Printed and bound in Poland; produced by Polskabook

British Library Cataloguing-in-Publication Data
A catalogue record for this book is available from the British Library

ISBN 978-1-903663-82-0

Contents

Factsheet

The Matrix	1999, USA
Running Time	136 minutes
Certificate	15
Production Companies	Village Roadshow Picture (Aus), Silver Pictures (US)
Distributor	Warner Brothers

Key credits

Writers/Directors	The Wachowski Brothers
Producer	Joel Silver
Production Designer	Owen Paterson
Director of Photography	Bill Pope
Music by	Don Davis
Editor	Zach Staenberg
Costume Designer	Kym Barrettdatabase)

Cast

Thomas Anderson/Neo	Keanu Reeves
Morpheus	Laurence Fishburne
Trinity	Carrie-Anne Moss
Agent Smith	Hugo Weaving
Cypher	Joe Pantoliano

Release strategy

Released in the USA on 2849 cinemas on 31 March 1999. Released nationally in the UK on 11 June 1999.

Synopsis

Computer hacker/software writer Thomas Anderson/Neo lives a discontented double life until he is contacted by a wanted man, Morpheus, who shows him he has been living inside an artificial computer simulation, the matrix. Instead of the year being 1999 it is 2199 and humans have become a power source and slaves to computers. Neo is believed to be 'the One' who can free the human race from the enslavement to the machines...

Budget

$63m

Introduction

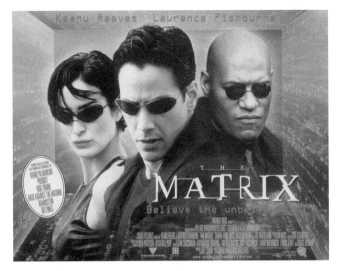

'What is *The Matrix*?' The tagline of the 1999 film, and the subsequent enigma of the film itself, brought audiences flocking to see a relatively unheralded mid-budget science fiction generic hybrid. So what exactly is it and what has been its appeal? Is it that it just looks so good, with its ice-cool costumes and techno soundtrack, sleek, slick characters who can fly, jump and manipulate time in ways we all literally dream about? Is it that the effects are so awe-inspiring that the 'wow' factor still sets it apart from its imitators years after its release? Or is it the film's self-conscious melding of the literary, religious, postmodernist, philosophical, filmic and even computer game aesthetic? *Studying The Matrix* asserts that it is this very combination as well as how the film does this that makes it so interesting to study, so endlessly fascinating to watch (repeated viewings are like

**peeling an onion – each time a new layer is exposed) and so
helpful in the study of film as cultural, generic and textual
construct.**

The power of the film can be seen in the alleged highest form
of flattery – imitation. It's groundbreaking 'bullet time' effects
have been parodied (with varying degrees of success) in films
such as *Shrek* (2001), *Charlie's Angels* (2000) and *Scary Movie*
(2000) and utilised by different media forms and genres across
the board (films such as *Equilibrium* (2003) display almost
shameless reliance on the vision of *The Matrix*). Not just the
special effects, but the then-new martial arts-influenced
action style has had a lasting and far-reaching impact
across film genres, influencing films from *Serenity* (2005)
to the *Bourne trilogy* (2002, 2004, 2007), and also the world
of computer gaming, both in terms of content and context.
Comic superheroes saving the world on our screens are now
regular fixtures on the yearly release schedule, from *Spider-
Man* (2002) to the *Fantastic Four* (2005 and 2007), in a sense
cultural responses to similar fears – one a fear of the future
in the pre-millennial *The Matrix*, whilst all since are arguably
responsive to fears of the present/shock from the past, post-
9/11.

So where did it come from? Its writers/directors the
Wachowski brothers (Larry and Andy) are former comic book
writers. It isn't hard to see what influence this has on *The
Matrix*. Neo is a glamorised 'hacker' come saviour rather
than computer nerd, in a sense a superhero in the making, as
powerful as Spider- or Superman blended with the spiritual
angst of Luke Skywalker. It is this stylistic edge in itself that
defines the output of the Wachowski's so far.

Prior to *The Matrix*, the brothers wrote and directed a small
budget ($5m) but impressive contemporary noir, *Bound* (1996).

A chic, stylish take on the genre, many of the thematic and visual elements of the film can be seen as precursors to *The Matrix* – costume, gender roles, names, sets and camerawork all bear similarities. It was, according to producer Joel Silver, 'an audition'[1] – before they were let loose with a $65m budget the studio had to see if they were up to it. In retrospect it is difficult to see that making *The Matrix* was a risky manoeuvre but looking at its intelligence and subtlety as well as its visual audacity, it is more than a cut above the standard Hollywood 'high concept' blockbuster. The film won Academy Awards for visual effects, sound effects, sound and editing – every category it was nominated for, as well as being the awards coveted by the much hyped release of the same year, *Star Wars Episode I: The Phantom Menace* (1999). Its worldwide box office was over $450m, making it up to that point the most successful film ever made by Warner Bros. and also helping to redefine the studio as making edgier, more sophisticated products.

What *Studying The Matrix* will attempt to do is look at the diverse influences behind and within the film, from its construction and intertextuality, its philosophical themes, iconographic use of costumes and effects, and star power to its industrial and ideological background. The broad concepts look at elements to be studied as part of both Film and Media Studies. For a more detailed look at the science fiction genre, Elaine Scarratt's Auteur book *Science Fiction Film: A Teacher's Guide to the Genre* (2001) is an excellent source of information and this is intended to dovetail into those themes specifically in relation to *The Matrix*.

By the end of 2003 the film had become part of an increasingly unsuccessful trilogy. Excitement and expectation was sky high for *The Matrix Reloaded*, with film magazines calling 2003 'the year of *The Matrix*', with a saturating marketing campaign and numerous ground-breaking tie-in products. Yet the critical and commercial success of the film was muted (as explored later in a specific chapter) and by the time *Matrix Revolutions* was released there was almost no anticipation for it. Ruminations on the failure of the two latter films could cite several different areas, from the diminishing returns of narrative and declining visual originality to lack of primary character development (as well as the introduction of a head-spinning number of new characters) and a po-faced over-seriousness. However, the first edition of this book was penned prior to the release of the sequels and, therefore, aside from an examination of *Reloaded*, the focus remains expressly on *The Matrix* itself. As by far the most ground breaking (and best) of the three it is the film that warrants exploration. Textually, however, much that applies to *The Matrix* can apply to the other two films. Hopefully it will prove transferable, useful, and in a *Matrix* sense, enlightening. It certainly has been to write it.

1 *The Matrix Revisited* DVD, 2001

1. Narrative

Looking at the narrative of *The Matrix*, one is not necessarily struck by its originality. Man is enslaved in the future to evil computers who use humans as their power source. A resistance fights to free the human race and searches for 'the One' who will be able to help them finally win the battle. Immediately it appears the plot borrows directly from the *Terminator* films (1984, 1991 and now 2003), as well as *Star Wars* (1977), and a whole host of others (considered in greater depth later). Before looking at specifics however, it is useful to outline key issues surrounding narrative and its relationship to genre.

Narrative generally means the ways in which stories are told. It has long been accepted that cultural and semiotic codes sit inside stories, seeing *myth* as the place where (in the case of cinema) what you are seeing and its cultural signification (*meaning*) join. French Structuralist Claude Levi-Strauss asserted that underneath individual stories lie the same myths. Each myth works in terms of 'binary opposition' – good/bad, dark/light – using opposites to make sense of contradiction and offering us ways of understanding society.

Critic Roland Barthes went one step further by asserting that cultural *signs* – from adverts to films to magazine covers – work towards making what is *ideological* (a constructed belief system) seem *natural*, therefore beyond questioning. These very concepts – the construction of myths to allow the dominant power to maintain authority without question – are what the narrative of *The Matrix* is concerned with. It seeks to make us question our assumptions as the world within the film most familiar to us is proved to be an artificial construct. In this case it is an artificial simulation, a myth.

Classical Hollywood narrative is the method by which the story and events within a film are linear. There is a sense of logical coherence, of cause and effect; there is conflict; and ultimately resolution, with all filmic elements working together to ensure continuity. This notion of resolution adheres to the overarching ideological purpose of myth. A story using such a code is normally formed in *three acts*. Todorov identified a standard formula within narrative of: Equilibrium – Disequilibrium – New Equilibrium[2]. This can be a useful basis for the examination of narrative – however it should not be seen necessarily as a prescriptive assumption, rather as a basis for deconstruction in a similar way to genre theory.

By breaking narratives down into scenes and acts it is possible to study how the narrative has been constructed on film. *Act One* is generally the setting up of the story in a state of equilibrium but ending in a climax leading to disequilibrium; *Act Two* will be the Development, with a Point of No Return in the middle and a climactic Moment of Truth at the end; with *Act Three* leading to a Final Climax[3], a point of new equilibrium. This structure is concerned with all elements working to allow for suspension of disbelief in the audience – even though they may know what they are seeing is not real, they still believe in it. However, science fiction film (as discussed in more depth under **Genre**, p.17) has specific thematic concerns, often with the nature of being human, the role of technology or anxiety over the future. As a genre, then, its narratives are often created to question the dominant ideology and myths, as *The Matrix* does. It is not necessarily concerned, therefore, with abiding by convention, or if it does, it may be in order to disrupt another. It is also fantastical, often using the future as temporal and spatial displacement, in order to question the present (again, see **Genre**).

The structure of *The Matrix* is interesting. A vital narrative element at the opening of any story is the hook. The *hook* in the case of cinema is something that happens early on to grab the attention of the audience and make them want to watch. In scriptwriting terms this 'hook' usually happens within the first five pages. In *The Matrix* it is achieved primarily visually through unexplainable actions – after Agent Smith (dressed as a superior law enforcement officer, tapping into cultural codes) states the police officers sent to arrest Trinity are 'already dead', the audience want to know how. Once Trinity jumps in mid-air, defying gravity and overwhelming all the officers, we are *hooked*. We want to know why, and even more how, it happened.

If the film is divided broadly into a three act structure, Act One could be said to be the opening of the film (a false equilibrium) through to Neo taking the red pill and awakening in his womb-like 'tank' in the real world and seeing it for the first time. However the audience, like Neo, still do not know what '*the matrix*' is and as such the film keeps us in suspense for a considerable period of time. With this it is worth considering the film's *mode of address* – how it addresses its audience. The presentation of the rebels, and of the matrix itself, is an *enigma* – it is a mystery, which the audience can enjoy attempting to solve, as is part of narrative pleasure.[4]

Act Two is when Neo (and the audience) learns about the matrix and his part to play (he is not a believer like the other characters, however, which allows him to consistently be the audience's main point of identification). His Point of No Return is arguably the crystallisation of his self-doubt when the Oracle tells him he is not the One. His Moment of Truth then comes with her prophecy –Morpheus sacrificing himself for Neo – coming true, leading him to return to *the matrix* and free him (in other words to believe for the first time), saving both Morpheus and Trinity and being forced to realise he may be the One after all. Act Three would then be his showdown with Smith, his death and his resurrection – becoming the One. But Neo does not truly believe until immediately before the film's end. His death also occurs concurrently with the imminent destruction of those in the real world, paralleling two interconnected stories for heightened dramatic effect. The film's end is also a beginning, and *The Matrix* has so many climactic moments that these broad structures are simultaneously adhered to and subverted. Its classical structure is undercut by the film's 'real' story remaining concealed until 30 minutes in, which could arguably divide the film into four rather than three sections.

It is important not to lose sight of the film's visual appeal and its frequent use of the *action code* (resolving or developing the narrative through action sequences) to develop the story, as well as the action movie's preoccupation with set-pieces. That events are often driven by their cinematic potential is a unique narrative element of cinema. It is worth noting the symbiotic relationship between narrative and genre at this point.

Following generic narrative codes for science fiction there are musings within the dialogue about the nature of man's dependency on technology. Russian writer Vladimir Propp identified the importance of character within narrative. He stated that there are 32 'spheres of action' for character functions, with coded character types (e.g. villain or hero) carrying common narrative functions. Morpheus (the donor/helper) is a philosophiser (as is Agent Smith to a certain degree), and, in keeping with the generic codes, these musings are often accompanied by impressive visuals to avoid any lull in narrative drive. That films such as *The Matrix* can critique the dominance of technology is ironic given the film's reliance on it – without the state-of-the-art special effects much of the visual power of the film would be lost (looked at in more detail under **Special Effects**). Neo may be the hero and Smith the villain but it is worth looking at these codes, specifically in relation to Trinity. She is not merely the hero's reward but a helper and indeed donor, offering the notion of social change (here the role of women) reflected in narrative.

As discussed in the section on *The Matrix Reloaded*, the sequel has multiple narratives across a range of media forms – greater understanding of the plot and minor characters in the film are fleshed out in the nine animated *Animatrix* shorts, as well as through the *Enter the Matrix* computer game. This is the first time a film's actual narrative has been part of a larger narrative across a range of cross-media platforms, creating a synergy of products and a meta-narrative, considered in more detail in the Institutions Chapter.

It is also of note that in some ways the narrative of *The Matrix*, as is now a general trend in big-budget action cinema overall, can at times be seen to emulate a computer game; for example, the lobby scene, as Trinity and Neo face a large number of guards, or Neo's fight with Agent Smith. Once more, this blurs the boundaries of cinema and therefore widens ideas of narrative to include the concept of highly adaptable and adept audience participation and consumption.

2 Rayner, Wall & Kruger, AS *Media Studies: An Essential Introduction*, 2001

3 Fensham, *Screenwriting*, 1996

4 Rayner, Wall & Kruger, ibid, 2001

2. Genre

Narrative, along with themes, settings, costumes, etc.,[5] all connote the codes that can be used to study genre. Genre theory was established in the 1960's – in part as a reaction to the development of the auteur theory – as an appropriate method for the study of films taking into account the texts and their meaning for audiences (partly due to the rise of cultural studies), as well as their place in wider industrial and social structures. Key genre critic Steve Neale's definition of genre as 'systems of orientations, expectations and conventions that circulate between industry, text and subject'[6] has been widely accepted. Genre is the recognition and meaning of similarities between texts in terms of a range of, for example, visual, character, narrative or thematic conventions, and their wider position as cultural texts: 'Genres can be approached from the point of view of the industry and its infrastructure...their aesthetic traditions...the broader socio-cultural environment upon which they draw and into which they feed, and from the point of view of audience understanding and response.'[7]

Genre's relationship to institutional practice is also visible in terms of film marketing. When selling a new film to an audience it can familiarise the unknown as well as identify and connect with an already established audience. Within genres are sub-genres – in the case of *The Matrix*, it sits most comfortably within the science fiction genre (i.e. thematically interested in science – discussed in more detail later) yet deals with artificial reality and digital technology (the *virtual reality sub-genre*), in common with a body of films thus forming a more acute method of deconstruction. It is also acknowledged that the boundaries of genre and genre theory do shift – *hybridity* (the melding of more than one genre within a text) is common in contemporary Hollywood cinema. In *The Matrix*, the film's playful referentiality/intertextuality with anything and everything from dialogue to camerawork categorises it generically but makes explicit its artificial construction. It fully acknowledges its role in the postmodern world of cultural imitation and replication. Thematically it borrows from a range of genres old and new, from high and popular culture alike.

In the broadest terms, *The Matrix* is a science fiction film offering a dystopian view of the future by exploring man's relationship to machine (as opposed to aliens). Filmic science fiction's roots have always been in literature, with many seeing Mary Shelley's seminal *Frankenstein* as the birth of the literary genre.[8] Writers like H.G. Wells at the end of the nineteenth century explored their concerns about the advancement of science. The Wachowskis have stated that influences on *The Matrix* are the science fiction novels of Philip K. Dick and William Gibson,[9] both of whose work has been adapted for the big screen (a Dick short story became *Minority Report* (2002) and Gibson penned *Johnny Mnemonic* (1995), which also starred Keanu Reeves).

A key element of science fiction literature and cinema is our relationship with **technology**. Another is temporal displacement – by using the future as a setting many contemporary issues can be played out. It allows us to explore anxieties about the increasing dependency we have on artificial intelligence (AI) and the encroachment of machines on the realms of humans. In *Frankenstein*, man's arrogance had him playing God and paying the price, the relationship of man to science representing man's interference with the natural order. This critique then becomes a moral one with man's creation (in this case artificially intelligent life superseding humans) wreaking its revenge. This symbiotic, dependent relationship is rendered physical in *The Matrix* as the humans take on elements of machines (the bolts in their arms, heads, spines, etc.), while the machines attempt to recreate a human world (the matrix itself) and must fight each other both within the matrix (the machine's 'turf' that Neo must learn to control) and the 'real' world (the human world still dominated by machines and technology). All the characters are fully versed and reliant on technology ('uploading' skills), using it to their advantage, further binding the fate of each to the other.

As mentioned, *The Matrix* has a similar 'back story' to that of the *Terminator* films – AI has overtaken humans as the dominant force, although whereas in the former the machines seek merely to annihilate the human race, in *The Matrix* they are bound to humans for energy. Like, again, the *Terminator* films, science fiction melds with action to create an event movie. Further, we should note the *intertextuality* within *The Matrix*. For example, when Neo emerges into the lobby and the camera shows him from the feet up in combat boots, the scene is reminiscent of the reverse scene in *T2* where the terminator comes down to the lobby to attack a host of soldiers. As Neo breaks Agent Smith's glasses one is reminded of the same scenario in *T2* where Arnold Schwarzenegger scowls at a nurse who breaks his shades. In the same fight scene, both Neo and Agent Smith run out of bullets, still holding their guns to each other's temples. This exact scene also appears in Robert Rodriguez's *Desperado* (1995) starring Antonio Banderas.

The Matrix may be science fiction at its core but it is a generic *hybrid*. It is a *bricolage* of a host of art forms, genres and influences, in the largest sense a blend of the action and technophobic science fiction film via the western, Hong Kong kung fu movies, film noir, John Woo, the virtual reality sub-genre, millennial angst, comic book superheroes, postmodernism, religions, classical mythology, 'cyberpunk', philosophy and a multitude of popular cultural texts from films to computer games. It is difficult to separate many of these diverse influences of *The Matrix* – one of the notably brave aspects of the film is its seamless ability to create something new out of what came before it. It alludes to a diverse range of other films as well as cultural texts and classical myth. The term 'cyberpunk' (does that phrase have any useful generic filmic meaning?) indicates succinctly the problems with categorising films by genre – the rules and boundaries are constantly being redefined.[10] Often zippy definitions of films are as much if not more about successfully marketing to an audience as calling into question the very limitations of genre theory. That *The Matrix* has as much in common with noir or science fiction noir (*Blade Runner* (1982), in particular) as it does with comic book adaptations (*X Men* (2000), for example) makes it ripe for study, exploring the shifting boundaries of film genres and its ramifications for audiences, institutions and the texts themselves.

As indicated, a further sub-generic concern of the technological anxiety science fiction film, *The Matrix* comes from a recent trend in science fiction concerned with the impact of digital technology as an interactive falsified experience – the *virtual reality sub-genre*. Reaching back to now-dated films like *Tron* (1982) and *The Lawnmower Man* (1992), both were in the early stages of looking at the ramifications of human/computer interactivity (in *Tron* a programmer is trapped inside a computer game and in *The Lawnmower Man* virtual reality is used to increase intelligence). Alongside concerns over man's relationship with technology in general, *The Matrix* is concerned with *simulation* and *virtual reality* and was released in 1999, the last year of the previous millennium, and along with films like *Strange Days* (1995) plays with those fears of the dawn of a new/end of an era and what that might mean. In *Strange Days* humans are able to relive/borrow experiences by wearing a headpiece which can record the experiences of another individual. The film's anti-hero, Lenny Nero (Ralph Fiennes) is an illegal trader of these experiences, similar to Neo as computer hacker (far 'cooler' than being a computer nerd, as discussed in the **Characters/Representation** section). In another film, *The Thirteenth Floor* (1999), humans have access to technology that can transport them to different eras via a computer simulation, with the central protagonist (responsible for the creation of the technology) eventually forced to realise he himself is a computer creation within a larger simulation. Keanu Reeves himself starred in a misfired William Gibson adaptation, *Johnny Mnemonic*, about virtual reality. Other films concerned with similar issues range from *Total Recall* (1990) to *eXistenZ* (1999) – directed by David Cronenberg, who also explored the relationship between the physical and the virtual/visual in *Videodrome* (1982).

With this concern over interactivity and immersion[11] comes, ironically, the suitability of such films either to represent or spawn computer games. This *cross-media fertilisation* in a sense juxtaposes the anxieties about the very nature of those experiences within filmic narratives of the sub-genre (that the media manufacturers are often owned by the same corporations should also not go overlooked). That the films themselves could play as **computer games** is another layer of their cultural capital, the difference being of course that with film the viewer still watches, unable to directly alter of control the direction of the narrative.

Another unavoidable influence is the **comic book** – the Wachowskis were previously comic book writers, explaining much of the visual impact of the film (they created staggeringly detailed storyboards).[12] Neo is a superhero. He has special gifts and powers, while Trinity is a leather-clad comic book heroine (with a twist – she is certainly not the over-sexualised busty babe of many comic creations). He can perform feats and stunts, he and his fellow characters wear costumes akin to a comic book but with a stylistic edge. We enjoy watching these superhuman feats identifying simultaneously with both his ordinary and extraordinariness. Tying in with the concept of *The Matrix* as heavily stylised and storyboarded is also the influence of Japanese animation ('anime') on the film – a style that inspired the film's oft-discussed bullet time effects.

Alongside the groundbreaking effects of *The Matrix* sit the stunts and action sequences, which are for the most part combat scenes, incorporating elements of the **martial arts** genre. Many of the showcases of the fighting and 'wow' factor effects adhere to the generic codes of the action movie – narrative is suspended, the scenes are wound into the story but have autonomy in the sensory pleasure they give the audience regardless of narrative coherence. That the contemporary generic tendency for Hollywood is the hybrid and that action/sci fi has almost become a genre in its own right can then be broken down further within *The Matrix* to non-Hollywood generic influences. The sequences of spectacle in the film involving the seemingly impossible – characters flying, moving against gravity, manipulating their environment through super human powers – are also found in Chinese martial arts heroes. The subtitled box office hit of the same year, *Crouching Tiger Hidden Dragon* (1999), draws on classical Chinese mythology as well as the martial arts of Hong Kong cinema to create a Hollywood film. Both films use extensive wire-work and shots of the actors performing their own stunts, as well as strong female fighting characters which are popular in Hong Kong movies. *The Matrix*'s kung fu trainer Yuen Wo Ping (who oversaw the lead actors – Reeves, Fishburne, Moss and Weaving – undergo over four months of martial arts training) was also used for *Crouching Tiger*, and whilst the films are opposed in their historical setting (one in the past, the other in the future) and use of weaponry (swords versus guns) they together predate the contemporary cinematic trend for the superhero comic book adaptations. *The Matrix* even goes so far as to offer a classical kung fu set-piece in the form of the sparring programme fight between Neo and Morpheus in which they fight within an oriental set wearing (co-ordinated) martial arts robes. These sequences are worked into the narrative so that the viewer will see a reason for their existence (in this case proving Neo's budding powers and Morpheus's role as mentor) but are in effect still moments of pure spectacle.

As well as the use of kung fu, and further unpacking the film's action element, the influence of celebrated action film-maker John Woo cannot be overlooked. His use of explosions, of slow motion and the visual feast they create has been knowingly incorporated into some of the film's most spectacular moments. Note that Woo's transference to Hollywood in a sense introduced elements of the martial arts film indirectly before either *Crouching Tiger* or *The Matrix*. In *Action/Spectacle Cinema* (2000), critic Jose Arroyo describes *Mission: Impossible* (1996) as 'glamorous, exciting, sexy and sometimes witty, I love the way it looks, and the gadgets and the clothes'. He could equally be writing about *The Matrix*. *Mission: Impossible* (directed by Brian De Palma) was seen as heavily influenced by Woo (who went on to direct *Mission: Impossible 2* (2000)), and it is hard not to credit the Wachowskis's use of slo-mo gunfire to the influential director.

'I know kung Fu.' The dojo / kung fu simulation

Woo also incorporates elements of the western, as does *The Matrix*, most notably with the fight between Smith and Neo (as did *Star Wars* with its intergalactic cowboys and duels). *The Matrix* also adds a splash of film noir to make it a hybrid genre film that alludes to the collision of a multitude of cultural conventions as diverse as they could possibly be. In addition are the numerous intertextual references within the film – *Night of the Lepus* (1972) playing on the TV screen in the Oracle's waiting room is a film about giant rabbits (referring, presumably, to *The Matrix*'s thematic concerns with *Alice in Wonderland*); an episode of cult TV show *The Prisoner* plays in the apartment Neo runs through – picking up on the parallels between the show's plot and that of *The Matrix*. There are also numerous references to *The Wizard of Oz* (1939) – calling Neo 'Dorothy' and referring again to the idea of two realities – black and white Kansas/colourful Oz, the desolate real world/the clinical matrix.

5 Scarratt, Science Fiction Film: A Teacher's Guide to the Genre, 2001

6 Neale, Genre, 1980

7 Neale, Genre and Contemporary Hollywood, 2002

8 Scarratt, ibid 2001

9 The Matrix Revisited DVD, 2001

10 Scarratt, ibid, 2001

11 King and Kryzwinska, Science Fiction Cinema: From Outerspace to Cyberspace, 2000

12 The Matrix Revisited DVD, 2001

3. Themes

'Welcome to the desert of the real': *The Matrix* and Postmodernism

Early on in *The Matrix*, when a client appears at his door, Neo/Thomas Anderson opens a book from which he takes an illegal disc. It is easy to miss, but the title of the book in question is recognisably *Simulacra and Simulation* (1981), a seminal cultural/philosophical text written by Jean Baudrillard. This is a key intertextual reference to arguably one of the strongest themes of the entire film. The phrase 'desert of the real', spoken by the film's philosophical commentator Morpheus, is a direct quote from the work. In interview Keanu Reeves has stated that before he could read the script for the film, the Wachowskis told him to read *Simulacra and Simulation*.

Baudrillard is concerned with the impact on culture when information is its key product – that is, that meaning and originality have been subsumed by imitation. But it is even more than this – he is not so much concerned with semiotics (the meaning of signs) – than with the *simulacrum*. This is a copy of which there is no original. This process, in which the difference between original and copy has collapsed, is the stage of *simulation*. Simulation is literally 'the generation by models of a real without origins or reality: a hyper-real'13, which is Baudrillard's view of postmodernity (Storey p. 163). The hyper-real is where simulation and reality are experienced as the same.

This whole notion, of what constitutes real or a simulation can easily be applied to cinema in general. Critics often discuss the level of 'realism' in particular film; historic events are depicted and film-makers strive for 'authenticity' when of course there can be none – a film is not 'real', it is a manufactured artefact projected onto a screen through a series of chosen images. It cannot be 'real', even if it attempts to reflect 'reality'. Yet despite this, film is one of the most powerful mediums in the postmodern world. Baudrillard's point was that what is not real (is simulation) can in fact seem more real than reality.14 It is a culture of borrowing, hence '**postmodernism**' has become a word used frequently and ironically often to the extent that it becomes a word almost without true meaning. That postmodernism is a 'buzzword' and that it involves the collapse of the boundaries between high and popular culture means that a popular film like *The Matrix* can tackle such questions. It is also worth noting that it is this cultural view that gives the greatest weight to the study of media and its forms.

On top of this theory is the idea that with the 'hyperreal' there is no actual truth. Everything in this scenario is formed out of myth. This is in opposition to the concepts of **modernism** – a search for true meaning. Whilst the matrix encapsulates the hyper-real, the 'real' world in *The Matrix* could be said to subscribe to the ideals of *modernism*. Everything becomes functional, reduced to basics, where the search for truth and meaning has led them. The chapter of *Simulacra and Simulation* that Neo opens is 'On Nihilism' (the belief in nothing) predicting the breakdown of civilisation experienced in the 'real' world. That Neo's name means 'new' also pertains to modernism – that which is new, original thought and learning.

Reflected even in the clothes they wear (which have no fashion purpose and are a form of *utopian dress* – see Street, 2001, p.89), the modernist ideals of this world stand in stark opposition to the artificial simulation which allows for excess. That the film relishes so much in the presentation of a hyperreal with all its trappings, from costume to actual playing with time on film ('bullet time' photography) and thus in people's eyes creates a tension. That which is concerned with the nature of the 'real' apparently celebrates both the wonders of the postmodern and yet renders it vacuous by being a prison. Thomas Anderson/Neo's search within *the matrix* is because 'there is something wrong with the world' – much of the discussion around the nature of the 'real' we hear from Morpheus and is straight from Baudrillard. The presentation of this theme is actually what drives the narrative. However *The Matrix* incorporates other philosophies – as with its generic hybridity, so too its thematic promiscuity.

'I expect you are feeling a bit like Alice...': *The Matrix* as Philosophical Allegory

The many references both explicit and implicit in *The Matrix* to Lewis Carroll's *Alice in Wonderland* and *Alice Through the*

Looking Glass are suitable metaphors for Neo's predicament, for he is lost and does not understand the cryptic nature of what he sees. Carroll's works have been read as allegories that discuss the nature of reality – for example in *Alice Through the Looking Glass* (the title alone a reference to mirrors, i.e. a metaphor for reflection on reality) Tweedledum and Tweedledee tell Alice that she is inside the Red King's dream and that if he stopped dreaming she'd cease to exist. That Neo takes the red pill after being referred to as 'Alice' can be seen as a direct nod in addition to the numerous further references and similar thematic concerns.

The Matrix is concerned with the very idea of perception; the notion that just because you see it/perceive it as real, how does one know that it is real? Much is made of the difference (or not) of dreams and reality, a concept which philosopher Rene Descartes discussed in depth. He was concerned with the nature of belief, of how we believe what our senses tell us and how these could be doubted and what that would mean. To disprove the certainty of believing the senses he refers to **dreaming**, a substantial theme within *The Matrix*. Morpheus states:

'Have you ever had a dream, Neo, that you were so sure was real? What if you were unable to wake from that dream? How would you know the difference between the dream world and the real world?'

This is based on the ideas of Descartes – that in dreams one experiences the senses as if one were awake (they can seem real) and it is only once awake that we know we were in fact dreaming15 in which case how do we separate them and know if either are in fact 'real'? This leads him to state that senses are therefore not a reliable enough system of proof for belief. 'For all we could ever know', Descartes concluded, 'the objective external world may not exist, all we can be certain of is our subjective inner life'.[16] Another aspect of the psychology of dreaming is that it allows for superhuman feats – dreams of flying are common. That time and space can be manipulated within the artificial world of *the matrix* equates it even more with a dreamlike state. It also allows for pleasure in the audience, of the powers one can have in a dream. Powers which, in reality, no one actually has (not even Neo in the real world). Morpheus, as the God of Dreams, has woken Neo, who can re-enter his dream and control it (something people often wish for). Metaphorical anxiety dreams are also represented – the idea of falling (Neo falls as he attempts to jump from one building to another) is tied to a fear of failure.

Descartes goes further than talk about the blurring between the dream and the real to meditate that there may be a 'malicious demon of the utmost power and cunning' who 'has employed all his energies in order to deceive me'[17]. His notion is that one can be tricked, and in a sense this is where the idea of *the matrix* comes from – humans are indeed being tricked, they are in fact in a permanent dream world being controlled not by a demon but by an artificial intelligence. Further writing has taken this idea and moved it forward – Peter Unger has suggested that instead of an evil demon we are being duped by a scientist who uses computers to produce electrical impulses. This would mean that we could not believe any of our experiences. Hilary Putnam goes even further, asking how do we know that we are not 'brains in vats', computer impulses telling our brains what to believe we are experiencing?

Another thematic concern of *The Matrix* is around the idea of the 'masses', of conformity and the predetermined nature of belief and ideology. As a democratic society, the west would seem to advocate individuality and self-worth. Yet the system of belief is taken as read, and is therefore difficult to oppose as power structures filter downwards to control in a sense the minds of its citizens. This is what Nietzsche called the 'herd mentality'[18] and unease about it is what Neo could be said to feel at the beginning of the film.

The idea of the conformity of the duped masses fits with Aldous Huxley's novel, *Brave New World*. Neo's search could be said to be for his individuality – a theme that the directors have acknowledged as blending with all the other influences. He could also be seen as a leader of a resistance to the dominant order of power, tapping into social movements which try and instigate change.

A further philosophical allegory to which *The Matrix* could be likened is Plato's parable of the cave, in which people are prisoners bound in chains within a cave and as such know no other existence. After one prisoner is freed he returns to the cave to explain to the others what he has seen (what the world is really like) and they do not believe him. In *The Matrix*, Morpheus warns Neo that 'most people are not ready to be unplugged', but Neo will go back to this 'cave' to show them.

The character of Cypher takes another stance. Where Neo, in taking the red pill, seeks the 'truth' and his 'true' self to escape the banality of his existence, Cypher, when faced with the harshness that comes with this truth, wishes to retreat back into the 'dream' world. This stance is a purely hedonistic one – where pleasure is the most important part of life.[19] However it is not real pleasure, and therefore cannot be meaningful, a component of true happiness in the self.

Ideologically, it is also worth considering why we unquestioningly side against the machines. They have done so much as to offer a world for humans to inhabit virtually (rather than merely leaving them in their 'tanks'), we learn that we humans ourselves 'scorched the sky' thereby presumably trying to annihilate the enemy that we created. The machines' point of view is described by Agent Smith, a 'human' face to the machines – it is 'their time'. Our ideological pre-programming as it were would have the humans as worth saving. Films can tap into such pre-existing cultural codes as short cuts to character definitions but can also question, within science fiction, the nature of these assumptions, in relation to myths and their role in maintaining (or questioning) dominant forms of power.

'There is no spoon': Religion and *The Matrix*

Neo is 'resurrected' by Trinity

Many of the names featured in the film are taken from classical mythology, indicating concerns with the nature of cultural myths. Many of these names and indeed themes of the film refer explicitly to the language and doctrine of Christianity (Neo as Christ resurrected, for example) and Buddhism. However the film is more pluralistic in its approach to religion than this, as it also incorporates philosophical and existential arguments within the narrative as well as references to literature (as previously mentioned).

As discussed later, Neo's predicament resembles that of Jesus – referred to continuously as 'the One', even as Jesus

Christ (see **Names** section), he is resurrected at the end of the film by Trinity. The film is littered with such Christian references. However 'the talent of *The Matrix* lies in its syncretic use of the philosophical and religious elements from various Western and Eastern traditions'.[20] Its depiction of a Messiah figure is not in keeping with Christianity – Neo is a crusader who uses any means (including violent means) to free the human race from enslavement rather than from damnation.

Christian belief also does not extend to the questioning of reality. It is sin that is to blame for the human condition in those terms. The nature of being and the search for true meaning involves the introduction of elements of Gnosticism (the search for spiritual knowledge), more in keeping with a religion such as Buddhism. The Wachowskis have stated that they were interested in Buddhism and where it meets with quantum physics – indicating their attention also to mathematics (represented by the code for *the matrix* itself in the film). In this sense, another theme is really about how we, humans, attempt to find answers to often unfathomably complex questions. They describe their faith as 'non-denominational'[21] which may partly explain the multiple influences on the film.

As with Christianity, however, these Buddhist themes are rendered explicit. As Neo can be seen as a Christ figure, so he can also be seen as a Buddhist Dalai Lama figure – also considered 'the One'. The iconographic use of mirrors (discussed in greater depth in **Iconography**) foregrounds one of the key elements of Buddhism – the importance of reflection in order to free oneself. Zen Buddhism advocates the practice of rendering one's mind as a mirror[22] in order to achieve a superior state unburdened by fear (Neo is told to 'free his mind'). The film's use of mirrors for this purpose becomes most explicit when Neo goes to visit the Oracle. There, among the gifted children who wait to see her sits a boy 'bending' a spoon. He is sitting in the lotus position and is dressed as a Buddhist monk (even without hair). His words indicate that he has found this true state:

'Do not try to bend the spoon. That's impossible. Instead only try to realise the truth...that there is no spoon. Then you will see it is not the spoon that bends, but yourself.'

Those four words, 'there is no spoon', are some of the directors' favourites in the entire film and one can see why – they encapsulate perfectly the very nature of the matrix and the search for freedom of the mind. That Neo sees himself in the spoon and that it bends not only displays the potential power he possesses but also means he is manipulating his own image – he can do this because the image is not real, and neither is the mirror which provides it. It epitomises that he is indeed bending himself.

Buddhism also guards against placing too much emphasis on the image – finding one's bliss in a sense becomes about letting go of it – something that Neo must do in order to fulfil his potential. Further Buddhist teachings emphasise 'direct experience as opposed to being held captive of the mind, and the need for constant vigilance and training'.[23] In keeping with the manifold thematic references to formal doctrines, however, *The Matrix* contradicts laws of Buddhism as it does Christianity. Buddhism preaches non-violence as well as the treatment of friend and foe alike. The film's killing of humans within *the matrix* asks us to conveniently sidestep such a contradiction and feast instead on the visual splendour. Religious purists may discount positive references due to the inclusion of such violence. Others may argue it aligns itself to the Civil Rights movement. However in the world of the action/

sci fi blockbuster few films have blended such disparate codes and theories to such unique yet popular ends. *The Matrix* can be read and appreciated on many levels, as pure action escapism or as a popular cultural artefact wrestling with the inherent contradictions that brings. The advent of postmodernism and its empowering of the popular allow such a film to be a melting pot of influences and meanings from all facets of social, cultural, philosophical and religious life.

13 Baudrillard, Simulacra and Simulation, 1981

14 Storey, An Introductory Guide to Cultural Theory and Popular Culture, 1993

15 Erion and Smith, Skepticism, Morality and The Matrix in The Matrix and Philosophy, 2002

16 Dreyfus & Dreyfus, The Brave New World of The Matrix, www.whatisthematrix.com

17 Descartes, The Philosophical Writings of Descartes, in The Matrix and Philosophy, 2002

18 The Brave New World of The Matrix, www.whatisthematrix.com

19 Erion and Smith, ibid, 2002

20 Brannigan, There is No Spoon: A Buddhist Mirror, in The Matrix and Philosophy, 2002

21 Interview with the Wachowskis, www.whatisthematrix.com

22 Brannigan, ibid, 2002

23 Brannigan, ibid, 2002

4. Film Language

Location/Setting

The majority of the sections in this chapter break *mise-en-scène* (everything within the framed shot) down into its components. Inevitably, thematic intent of science fiction has great bearing on setting. As 'science fiction distances science and society in time and place in order for us to see our contemporary society more clearly'[24], this displacement allows challenging critiques for which a most suitable setting/series of settings may be chosen. Whilst some science fiction narratives may pitch utopias against dystopias, *The Matrix* interestingly pitches two dystopias against each other – the matrix is a device enslaving humans, but the freer 'real' world is a cold and dangerous place where pockets of rebellion hide from destruction. The sensibilities of both are at opposite ends – in the former, life carries on for everyone, working and living under the guise of post-industrialist capitalism. In the latter, all individual needs are subordinate to the goal – the destruction of the matrix. The narrative drive has this as the concept of a utopia – re-establishing freedom for the human race in the form of modernism and enlightenment.

Clearly the two main settings of *The Matrix* are the matrix itself as artificial construct, and the 'real' world. For the audience, it is paradoxically the matrix that bears the closest relation to reality, a concept fundamentally intertwined with the film's thematic concerns of simulation. In representing the matrix, the film is not however representing reality but a false construction of it that can pass as real enough to its inhabitants (and viewers until we, like Neo, learn the 'truth'). That the setting of the matrix is not real displaces spatially and also temporally (it is set in the past, our present) the location, tying in with the notion of critiquing our world by displacement. That there is no other planet featured immediately brings closer the concerns of the film as about our world, and our race, itself a utopian ideal where racial tensions and power struggles are subsumed by the common bond of being human.

The matrix is presented within the film as a **city**. It is notable that the majority of science fiction landscapes are urban, 'especially cities where technological progress and business are more visible'.[25] These environments range in appearance but the concept is the same. A human rather than natural construct with particularly the CBD (Central Business District) homage to man's technological and architectural prowess, a city is potentially a microcosmic representation of society as a whole. Commerce and capitalism reign in their busy centres, manmade endeavour forever in a hurry. These large, towering centres (skyscrapers are another key iconographic element of the sci fi urban landscape) can also be read as denoting the alienation of human beings from their natural roots, and the isolation of the individual –surrounded by many, knowing few, and in the face of such inconsequentiality, lacking/seeking true meaning – the postmodern condition rendered visual, as it were. The role of technology and its prominence in cities and opposition to nature (therefore rural settings) are another important factor where the film's theme relates to technological anxiety as embodied by this backdrop.

Visually as well as thematically, the use of an Australian cityscape (Sydney) in substitute for the oft-filmed cities of the USA has quite a major impact on the appearance of the film, rendering it familiar (a city) yet cinematically unusual (a displacement). The sandstone buildings work well alongside the desired coloured hues of the artificial world. The directors have stated that it was filmed there for financial reasons, but it also adds much to the innovation of the film. It certainly helps differentiate *The Matrix* once again as being visually unique in multiple ways, and potentially therefore slightly alienating rather than familiar to the cinema-goer (a key concept of *the matrix* as 'unreal'). Despite the use of a non-American city, however, they wanted it to appear to be a generic city in the USA therefore much time and energy was spent altering street signs, etc. to allow for this (for example in Australia, like in the UK, they drive on the left, unlike the USA). Incidentally, the junctions called out as phone locations within the matrix are street names from Chicago, the Wachowskis' hometown. The city in *The Matrix*, therefore, becomes a construct of multiple cities and identities, an 'every city'.

The Matrix makes full use of its urban space to spectacular effect. The skyscraper does not merely have symbolic meaning, it is key in several set-pieces. Neo climbing out onto the window ledge and looking down; Neo and Trinity fighting agents on the roof; Trinity flying Morpheus and Neo to safety by dropping them on the roof of a skyscraper; and finally a helicopter crashing into one, in a scene that now bears unavoidable premonitions of 9/11. As with the iconographic technology, the symbolic is interweaved seamlessly with seeming narrative necessity.

Everything within the world of *the matrix* is tinged with **green**. All the costumes were partially dyed with green, the lighting tinges green on most of the surfaces, Neo's apartment door is green, and the book he retrieves his disks from is green as is Agent Smith's file, all of which gives it a stylised other-worldliness. Only on close inspection can one see large sheets of green mesh hanging over in the background as, for example, the characters walk or run through Sydney's streets – presumably used to hide shop frontage that would be too 'real', which they do successfully as well as emphasising also the green tinge.

The other colour used sparingly and to dramatic effect is **red**. In its boldest forms it is the red pill that Neo swallows and his attention is caught by 'the woman in the red dress' shortly after the red man turns green on the pedestrian traffic lights as he walks through a simulation with Morpheus. The primary colour has a range of cultural meanings – red for danger, blood red – which when placed against the green hue makes it all the more spectacular.

The use of **grids** in the sets can be seen throughout. It deliberately gives *the matrix* a constructed, mathematically precise effect, from the symmetrical sterile hell of Neo's cubicle and the corner office to the floor or ceiling tiles in Neo's interrogation room, the room where Morpheus is held captive to the windows of the skyscrapers and pillars in the lobby scene. The linear, constructed nature of the sets greatly flatters the idea of *the matrix* as a cold, artificially constructed simulation where organic humans have adapted rather than seem to fit, a further social critique visually rendered.

Opposingly, scenes within *the matrix* featuring the Resistance members can have a classical grandeur – the room where Neo meets Morpheus for the first time is replete with imposing high contrast black and white tiled staircase, period windows, marble fireplace and red leather chairs offering an atmosphere of faded grandeur and history. The chairs reappear in the training programmes, which offer alternative locations, most startlingly the classical, Oriental forum for the dojo/kung fu fight, made up of sepia walls and wooden beams (co-ordinated with the characters' costumes).

The post-apocalyptic wasteland that the rebels inhabit in the 'real' world is only shown in wide shot a few times in the film and is the antithesis of a rural idyll, the dystopia of the 'real' being that both the rural and the urban human societies have been destroyed and no longer exist. First, Morpheus shows Neo the true 'look' of the city today, destroyed and destitute. He does this through a computer simulation however, as he does to show Neo (and the audience as the scenes are straight-to-camera) the fields where humans are grown. We do not actually see the real world apart from the sewers where the Nebuchadnezzar plays cat-and-mouse with the Sentinels. That they inhabit the sewers says much about the state they have been reduced to. As images we have little concept of their size or geography, making them unfamiliar and, alongside the darkness above due to the human-induced 'scorched sky', add to the dank, subterranean ambience that humans have been forced to inhabit. The design of the ship and Sentinels offer key iconography into the foreign creations of the machines, heightening the sense of danger within the unsafe 'real' world. That the 'real' world is tinted blue by lighting and background stresses the cold, desolate atmosphere they inhabit and aptly contrasts the green hue of the matrix simulation.

There could be said to be a third location – the computer programme in which Morpheus induces Neo into the ways of *the matrix*, from the kung fu fighting sequence to where Neo and Trinity get their guns. This is 'their' space, their computer programme. They are able to use and manipulate technology for their own aims – what the computers are arguably doing to humans in the real world. It is also a place where fights and visual set-pieces can occur in safety, away from genuine danger.

The sheer contrast of the destroyed civilisation to the pristine order of *the matrix* vitally infuses further urgency to the struggle of the resistance. For the most part the location in the real world is inside their craft, the Nebuchadnezzar. It is a far cry from *Star Trek* – the 'insides' of the ship are on the 'outside' – everywhere there are cables. The ship has an organic quality, looking somewhat cobbled together and unfinished, permanently changing and under construction – a look that the production designers specifically wanted. The old and the new seem to blend in the sense that the computer screens and access to technology they have (from which they can 'learn' instantaneously skills such as kung fu) sit juxtaposed with worn-looking metal constructions more black than the usual gleaming metallic chrome used in traditional sci fi spacecraft. Use of shallow focus blurs backgrounds making them softer and allowing the characters to appear more prominent, in keeping with the real world scenes emphasis on the humans and a modernist sensibility.

Iconography

Iconography describes 'any cultural image which has powerful resonance, or which encapsulates or embodies an aspect of culture or an idea'.[26] There are many standard types within certain genres (long trench coats, guns and *femmes fatale* in film noir, for instance) and the pervasive use of signs within western culture leads to the potential for semiotic study both within *The Matrix* and its self-conscious appropriation of these

'We're going to need guns ... lots of guns.'

lasers or light sabres, *The Matrix*, in keeping with its use of contemporaneous iconography, does not.

Rendered a necessity to help the resistance fight the machines, the use of guns creates a spectacular 'slo-mo bullet-fest'[27] on multiple occasions. Debate about gun ownership and the havoc it wreaks is bypassed somewhat by the displacement and digital manipulation of its use for spectacle. The visual pleasure gained from the beauty of slow motion bullets in the air or exploding on impact with pillars of 'marble' is difficult to equate morally with the destructive force in reality that is the gun, touching on areas of the media violence debate. When the Resistance fight their enemies in the matrix they are shooting policemen rather than Agents – killing 'real' people, those they are trying to free. That they are not in fact real bullets does not matter as we know the 'body cannot live without the mind' and once a person is killed in the matrix, they die in the real world. This is never addressed directly within the film. In keeping with the idea of a comic book world, perhaps the inference is that the violence is not real and is displaced due to the genre being science fiction. It is a fertile area for debate.

There is enormous range in the type of guns used in *The Matrix* – they use just about every type, from handguns to shotguns to automatic machine guns and at one point, in a moment of pure tongue-in-cheek excess, an enormous machine gun attached to a helicopter. It could almost be seen as a celebration of the gun in all its forms. Despite the variety it is notable that every single one, as with other iconographic elements of technology in the film (from mobile phones to costume), is black, as is the helicopter in the rescue scene.

The special effect desginers on *The Matrix* introduced 'bullet time' technology and indeed there is also on several occasions a specific focus on the **bullets** themselves afforded by this style of photography (as empty shells fall from guns and the helicopter or most notably as Neo stops bullets mid-air following his resurrection). Incidentally the Wachowskis used this technique to a lesser extent in their first film, *Bound*, when one character is shot whilst standing in a pool of paint.

In one key scene, the lobby assault, guns and costume work together – Neo's overcoat conceals a veritable arsenal of weaponry and as their bullets move in slo-mo so do their long coats (covered more in the section on **Costume**). The sheer irrefutable 'coolness' of this sequence is enhanced by their throwing away of guns once used – guns may have been irrevocably linked to movies in Hollywood for decades, but seldom have they been discarded (rendered disposable and dispensable) with such gleeful panache. Add to that the almost constant reappearance of yet *more* guns of different type to vary sound, speed and thus pace of the scene in their wake and the sheer excess of the entire sequence and guns become invaluable to the staging of the film itself. As stated, ironically, the majority of the film's ocular gratification is from presentation of action in the matrix – without it, much of the film's power would be lost.

The representation of **technology** is of course vital to the preoccupation of *The Matrix*, as with much of science fiction here it is tied to machinery and its impact on human civilisation. The matrix itself is a representation of the possibilities of technology in the future, but in terms of iconography recognisable to us, the majority of it comes from the film's depiction of computers and machines.

In keeping with the coloured hue of the artificial matrix, the font used to depict the code for the matrix is **green**. That it is on black screens is in keeping with the prevalence of that colour within the film (and the overtones it brings with it) but is also the style actually used by older computers in the 1980s. This was deliberate, 'inspired by the phosphorous green of old PCs'[28] and offers a retro-chic to the technology as well as being the most striking way to display the code. The film is both introduced and almost concluded with green writing on a black screen, from which the camera zooms (impossibly) into the digit or letter itself, embodying the three-dimensional world housed within/beyond the computer code (the matrix).

This is not the only time a screen becomes a three-dimensional image, as it were. As we first see Neo sitting in the interrogation room, it is on a surveillance screen. The camera zooms towards the screen and, with the aid of sound and visual effects, goes through the screen to enter the room. The image seems to become real; a conceit played on heavily within the film, but of course Neo in the interrogation room is not real. Screens, images and the whole notion of seeing are paramount as, in a sense, the film refutes the idea that 'seeing is believing' – the very nature of the image can lessen meaning and disguise what is 'real'.

Mirrors are another key motif. That they reflect means that the image one sees on them is not real, embodying key concerns of the film, that of the confusion of the image with the real. The directors have stated that 'reflections in general are a significant theme in the film' and show 'the idea of worlds within worlds'.[29] Their use also ties in with a Buddhist reading of the film (as described in the section on **religion** and the film) – a state for the mind to aspire to is that of a mirror, merely reflecting, then in an ideal state to have no mirror – to have reflected and reached a bliss-like state of being.

For example: we see action in a rear-view mirror as Trinity watches Neo's arrest from her motorbike; we see Neo in Morpheus's glasses as he decides between taking the red or blue pill (the two lenses not only 'reflecting' his choice but representing his two possible paths); and we see Neo's face reflected in the car window as he drives through *the matrix* to see the Oracle (aware for the first time that *the matrix* is not real). The latter scene also uses rear-projection to blur the images outside the car – Neo's face and those in the car are crisp while the external view is out of focus – another deliberate manipulation of image to bring to the fore questions of the 'real'.

Other occasions where mirrors feature include the mirror moving after Neo has taken the red pill – demonstrating a literal blurring of image and reflection with reality, a collapse of the two moments before he wakes up in the 'real' world. The mirror moves along his arm onto his body, taking him with it, and in this sense the mirror becomes him/he becomes the mirror. That all the aforementioned reflections involve the central protagonist is key – each time they reflect a moment in Neo's metamorphosis, from being meekly escorted out of a building by agents to his encounter with his own image in the back of a spoon that can bend because 'there is no spoon' (a Buddhist allegory). Added to this are the reflective materials of some of the costumes (noticeably *not* Neo's) and the emphasis in shine and sheen in the clinical world of the matrix (marble pillars, windows etc) combining to depict a world reflecting itself with little meaning other than for the look itself. Incidentally one of the most dramatic moments involving mirrors in the film is when the helicopter collides with a skyscraper, the windows of which resemble mirrors. That it causes the whole structure to warp and dramatically explode might be read as symbolising the destruction of the image.

One of the ironies of the film is that the matrix, the world we recognise the most, is not real whilst the 'real' world bears little resemblance to ours – futuristic, desolate and hostile. Where machinery and its relationship to man stems from the themes of the film, the machinery presented as 'real' for the Nebuchadnezzar hovercraft (covered in **Settings/Locations**), the Sentinels, the bugs, etc., all come from conceptual art (by comic book artist Geoff Darrow) and are fantastical to us. Part of the fascination of science fiction comes in the presentation of the 'gadgets', and apart from the 'Neb', the futuristic machines resemble insects. The Sentinels, 'squiddies', look like just that, their movements graceful as they find their prey. Once aboard the Neb near the end of the film, as they peel through the ship's hull to get inside, their underbelly displays dozens of small legs moving frantically. Associations of insects, particularly cockroaches etc., are often negative, even phobic, and using these shapes taps into those pre-existing cultural fears and views. (That the 'bug' they plant in Neo turns into an actual bug is another nod to dual word meanings/an 'in-joke', also used for comic effect in *Men in Black* (1997).)

The **telephone** and **mobile phones** become pivotal in the film as they link the real world to the matrix and allow the character within each at any one time to be in contact. 'Communication devices are particularly effective in creating dramatic tension because if they fail, characters become isolated and vulnerable' (Scarratt, 2001). A good example of this is where Neo is left alone to face Agent Smith for the showdown after the phone's receiver is destroyed. This obviously does not merely apply in science fiction films – many pivotal, classic cinematic scenes have revolved around telephones. The phone linked Corky and Violet in neighbouring apartments as they scammed the mob in the noir *Bound* so once again the directors use it as a device. The phone takes on more importance however in *The Matrix* as a portal between the artificial and the real via an old fashioned phone line, resonant of the pre-broadband method of 'dialing up' to the Internet. There are multiple occasions in the film where phones, both 'hardlines' and mobiles, become pivotal to the plot. Conversations, wires, codes all offer up artificial forms of communication and therefore potential misuse. The telephone is the first indication of Cypher's betrayal we have – at the beginning, as we hear Trinity talking to Cypher, we/she hears noises and asks if the phone is tapped. He replies no, but she is then surrounded by police/agents. Later, when he traps the resistance, he does so by dropping his mobile outside their meeting building allowing them to be traced. It is how Morpheus first contacts Neo to warn him of the Agents' arrival and how Neo finds a new exit at the end of the film. Anxiety about the impact of mobile phones is subsumed by them appearing as desirable commodities (again the colour black). Both through the use of the idea of virtual reality via the internet and the power of mobile phones the film mobilises current technology for new means. It also raises issues of product placement, with the mobiles used being visibly Nokia hand sets.

The original film's foregrounding of the use of mobile phones encapsulating technological advancement is still there but less overt in *Reloaded*. The arrival of 3G mobiles, with picture and video advances accelerating to sustain growth in an already saturated market place would leave technological representation dated quickly. The first film's setting of 1999 will presumably be the same for *Reloaded* and *Revolutions*, therefore putting them in a difficult position – by ignoring modern advancements the films may alienate technology-conscious audiences, but by including them they lose the focus on a pre-millennial setting. It will be worth examining whether the focus on mobiles diminishes further.

Costume

The importance of fashion and costume in film as a site of meaning has often been neglected, viewed as 'a frivolous, feminine field, one of the primary ways in which women are trapped into gratifying the male gaze'.[30] Yet as a part of film language they can greatly contribute to the overall look of a

film and thus have a significant effect on the *mise-en-scène* as well as carry with them pre-existing cultural codes. Costume can act as a signifier and therefore have an important effect on narrative as well as visual elements of a film.

Science fiction films in particular can make full use of the language of costume as they need not abide by rules of realism but can indulge

Costume in The Matrix *contributes greatly to the feel of the film*

in excess and innovation. In terms of spectacle, costume can enhance audience pleasure and engagement at a visual level and create literally 'iconic clothes'.[31] *The Matrix* is an excellent example of this, using costumes that draw attention to themselves and contribute greatly to the overall look and feel of the film (in the dojo fight scene for example organic costume colour co-ordinates with set dressing).

In terms of female costuming in science fiction, it has been used previously to display the female body as sexual object (for example Jane Fonda's space-age outfits in *Barbarella*, (1968)). It could be easily argued that *The Matrix* conforms to such an ideal, with its leading female clad in skin-tight black PVC. This would, however, be an oversimplification as, as with much of the film in general, more than one meaning can be ascribed and the film plays heavily on disrupting and reassigning codes.

As described previously, *The Matrix* is arguably a critique of the image-saturated postmodern world where the 'real' has lost all meaning. The two worlds within the film, the 'real' world and the matrix itself, are coded visually as well as culturally as polar opposites, and the costuming within the film reflects this juxtaposition. In the 'real' world, characters wear shapeless grey jumpers and outfits, with the clothes appearing entirely functional and without fashion. This world is without the image-consciousness of the postmodern matrix. However one of the ironies of the film is that whilst the destruction of the matrix will lead to freedom and a permanent state of the 'real' (the more utopian of two dystopias, as it were), the vast majority of the pleasure of the film for the audience is in witnessing events within the matrix itself. It is there that the excess – from the bullet time photography to the leather-clad Trinity – can be exploited and where the 'cool' look of the film is set.

It is within the matrix also that much of the film's play with genre and gender can be seen and costume plays a significant part of this. Coding differing elements of both femininity and masculinity through costume is used as a sign of self-awareness and power within the film (the Wachowskis also used it in *Bound* to connote the differing femininities of characters Violet and Corky). Neo, for example, as Thomas Anderson in the matrix, wears non-descript clothing to work (brown) and only once his confidence has grown within the real world can he enter the matrix looking as sharply dressed as the others (i.e. his 'residual self-image' has altered irrevocably). A key scene for this transformation of Neo (from Neo as self-doubter to self-believer) is as he and Trinity return to the matrix and enter the lobby where Morpheus is being held. Neo's long, wool coat (note that it is not leather – Neo never wears shiny textures unlike Trinity or Morpheus) and big military-style boots, from which the camera tilts upwards, bring to mind the heavy duty masculine imagery of the lobby scene in *Terminator 2* (Schwarzenegger wears boots and leathers and is also shot from the feet up in more than one occasion as he, similarly, takes on multiple law personnel). However, here Neo's costume could be said to be sending up such macho dress as his coat is being used to disguise his plethora of weapons and also, like Trinity's PVC coat, moves elegantly as the two cart wheel in slow-motion.

Kym Barratt, the costume designer for the film, talks about 'iconoclastic silhouettes that give you a certain subconscious feeling about what's happening quickly'. This is clearly visible in the lobby scene. She also describes how much time was spent testing how different fabrics moved in the air, how they would reflect the light (a key point particular in terms of Trinity) and on technical elements such as how they could conceal harnesses, wires and even fibreglass plates (to keep the actors straight when flying through the air). She states her instructions from the directors were 'We want it to be dark, we want it to be high contrast, we want Trinity to be like an oil slick'. The use of the colour black brings with it associations – of power, of sophistication and seriousness, as well as introducing elements of noir, a genre well know for creating high-contrast visual images. Trinity's specific 'oil slick' look is arguably pleasurable to the male gaze, however (as discussed in more detail in the character analysis) whilst the tightness of her costume exposes her silhouette and highlights her form for her bullet time stunts (particularly important for the impact of her/the film's first one), it also conceals her body (never showing more than either her arms or her shoulders) and in the form of actress Carrie-Anne Moss offers an androgynous rather than highly feminised look.

Another key to the iconographic costuming is in the importance of **accessories**. These are primarily sunglasses (again connoting 'coolness' alongside the costumes), mobile phones and guns. Sunglasses, as well as enhancing further the glamour and mystique of the costumes, also conceal the eyes – they are even used as mirrors particularly by Morpheus reflecting back the look. All are black, in keeping with the 'look' of the resistance (sleek). Both the phones and sunglasses are easily copied as fashion items in our real world – much was made by Nokia on the film's release of its use of their phones, and there even exists a website where you can purchase 'Matrix shades'.

Special Effects

The role of special effects within both the spectacle and narrative of science fiction/action films is contentious. It could be argued that by dazzling an audience with big-budget CGI effects, other elements of the film – narrative and characterisation for example – can be weaker, or can even be excuses for these spectacular displays. However such arguments are not straightforward. Within most science fiction films will be a discourse about the role of technology. Whilst there can be no doubt that audiences enjoy the visual splendour of awe-inspiring effects, cinema in general, particularly the 'event' movie (increasingly science fiction/ comic book based), is designed as a sensational experience. That effects can heighten this is merely an extension of a visual medium. Added to this is the interesting juxtaposition of critique and celebration – whilst thematic and narrative concerns may critique the encroachment of technology onto the human existence, the genre itself constantly pushes the boundaries of technological achievement.

As discussed in **Genre**, one of the key elements of science fiction is the special effects. A film set within a virtual reality/ computer programme designed to look like our world offers huge scope for playing with the laws of gravity, time and super-human abilities and the spectacular cinema that old create. The technical team behind the film have recounted the attempts by the directors to describe the effects they wanted – how they went to ILM (Industrial Light and Magic – the effects house owned by George Lucas) and were turned away and how they happened upon a far lesser known company, Manex, who provided the necessary prowess and vision.[32]

Continuing the comparison between *Terminator 2* and *The Matrix*, both have offered groundbreaking special effects. In *Terminator 2* it was the liquid metal cyborg's shape-changing that foregrounded CGI (computer generated imagery) developments. With *The Matrix*, it is the invention of '**bullet time**' photography, the likes of which had not been seen on film before to such astonishing effect. On a basic level it is

'Bullet time' special effects in action

a camera technique which breaks the standard **180-degree rule** – the rule that means scenes should be filmed from the same side to avoid the character jumping from one side of the frame to the other. In bullet time the camera can move at 360 degrees, highlighting the action and offering, along with the effects, dramatic action sequences.

Key moments in *The Matrix* where bullet time technology is used are:

- Trinity's opening fight scene as she jumps, suspended in midair;

- Neo dodging an Agent's bullets on the roof;

- Morpheus being shot in the leg trying to escape from the skyscraper;

- The western-style showdown between Neo and Agent Smith.

The phrase 'bullet time' was coined by the Wachowski brothers. Previously the technique was know was 'flo mo', and was designed by the film's visual effects supervisor, John Gaeta, with his company Manex that specialised in motion control photography. Scenes where bullet time was to be used were simulated inside computers, 'blocked' using the actors and standard cameras, then the data was combined to show the path needed for each shot in 'bullet time'. The concept involved placing up to 120 still cameras on a mapped path on a specially designed adjustable 'rig' that could be moved to form a variety of shapes and camera heights (curves at 360 degrees or example, as with Agent Smith and Neo's subway fight or Neo dodging bullets on the roof). Each camera was triggered to go off at different times (the frame rates varying from 100 to 2000 frames per second).[33] As the actors moved on wires, the cameras could photograph the action from different points of view at different times – in other words leaving slight gaps in time between the shots, and able to capture action from multiple points of view in a way conventional film cameras could not possibly manage to do. Films are only ever still images played so fast that they look to be fluid, but the camera can only move so quickly. What was happening here was that in addition to the multiple possibilities for camera angles, the gaps in time/frames could be manipulated to suspend the normal rules of time and gravity. It also meant that the cameras could be mapped in a way that they change direction (or even stop on one point, as with Trinity in the opening sequence).

Such images were computerised, 'motion estimation/ interpolation' used to animate between the frames by analysing the pixels in each individual frame. In effect the technique is the same as full cell animation except this uses real people, animating around them to slow down time, stretch movements all the while maintaining crisp imagery for the viewer. The technique in effect combines stop motion photography with digital animation, allowing for characters to move at different speeds.

Alongside these constructed sequences were virtual backgrounds – three-dimensional sets scanned into a computer that would allow virtual cameras to go literally anywhere, not restricted by physical space. Such computer generated sets are used in fully computerised animations such as *Monsters Inc.* (2001), but the difference here is that the sets are based on what is 'real' and designed to look 'real'. *The Matrix*'s virtual sets came with virtual lighting and cameras, able to enhance further the potential offered by placing each character-centred bullet time stunt very much within a highly manipulated background.

Bullet time photography may be seen as the most audacious effect in the film, however other shooting and post-production effects within the matrix involved similarly time-consuming efforts. For example the pivotal 'lobby scene' in which Trinity and Neo walk into a government building and proceed to demolish it took a week and a half to shoot[34] and involved wire work, exploding foam pillars (painted to look marble) and a bomb exploding, much of which had to be enhanced at the post-production stage. The biggest explosion in the film must surely be the helicopter crashing into the skyscraper, spectacle achieved by the glass bending and warping (almost like water – some of the film's effects do indeed seem to appear underwater in their grace and fluidity) before smashing violently.

In terms of further photographic trickery, another notable scene is the 'woman in the red dress'. As Neo and Morpheus walk against the crowd and Neo spots a woman in a scarlet satin dress, Morpheus freezes the scene. The effect is incredible, as they stand, talk and walk around frozen people and, most stunningly, a water fountain. Three versions of the scene were short – a blank background, the fountain at 96 frames per second rather than 24 (making it ultra-clear), and the people – and then combined. The definition of the shot is crystal clear, another element contributing to its 'wow' factor.

Not to mention, of course, the CGI creations such as Neo's mouth disappearing, the 'bug', Neo's hallucinations as he touches the mirror after taking the red pill and the numerous effects within the computer simulation training programmes – the kung fu / dojo fight, the 'jump programme', 'guns, lots of guns' and countless others. Each of these effects elements is seamlessly merged with stunts, photographic, cinematic and digital camera work, editing, colour, costume and sound to produce a dazzling spectacle integrating the 'real' with the seemingly impossible, embodying and utilising the film's overarching themes of reality and simulation.

It is easy to focus on the bullet time effects and those within the matrix and miss out the fact that the 'real' world also consists of vast numbers of CGI scenes and creations. The Sentinels as well as the Neb, the scorched city and the fields of growing humans are all artificially created and add to the contrast of reality/simulation. As with the iconography common to science fiction the presentation of technology is coherent and is accompanied by sound effects to render what is not real believable.

Sound

Sound is overall a vastly neglected area of film study. Its potential to shape ambience, create and dissipate tension and assign melodies and motifs to familiarise characters should not be overlooked when studying film as a constructed text. In science fiction sound is particularly crucial – it can make what is not real (digital effects, for example) seem real.

In science fiction film, sound effects have to be created for things that do not actually exist – spacecraft, weaponry, gadgets, etc. In the 'real' world of *The Matrix*, this means the rebel ship, the sentinels, the machines controlling the human-growing 'fields', the 'EMP' being used, the sounds for insertion into the skull of the virtual reality spike, etc. All of these involve the creation of 'real' noises for what does not exist. Learning about these can be tremendous fun as the origins of the super-advanced sounds can often be incredibly simple (a microphone being dangled next to a television's cathode ray tube as a light sabre noise in *Star Wars* for example, or England's cricketing 'barmy army' chants used for Saruman's army march in *The Lord of the Rings: The Two Towers* (2002)). The priority in science fiction is to make it all seem believable, no matter how fantastical.

In *The Matrix*, sound and soundtrack could easily be overshadowed by the film's visual power, but cleverly the film uses both in close conjunction. During the opening sequence when we see 'bullet time' for the first time as Trinity jumps on the air, hits and kicks her way through a group of dim-witted policemen, the 'wow' factor of the moment is enhanced by both costume (shiny, foregrounding her silhouette – as discussed in the **Costume** section) and sound. Sounds Effects Supervisor of the film, Dane Davis (who won an Oscar for the film) explained that the sound department spent much time creating thousands of 'whoosh' sounds to play backwards, distort, etc. for the sounds of the combat.[35] The sound Trinity's limbs make as they hit and kick in the air are a good example of how the film styled these sounds on kung fu movies but went much, much further to create multiple sounds for enhanced effect – body hits, face hits, moving limbs, etc. (there are several other 'key' scenes where these noises are prominent – the kung fu fight between Morpheus and Neo, the fight on the skyscraper roof and the 'showdown' between Smith and Neo). Also notable in the opening is that when

Trinity runs along the wall, gunfire accompanies (in precise synchronisation) her steps, creating a punchy power to her movements. As she jumps from one building to the other, a police siren sounds and changes pitch perfectly synchronised with her movements, bending sound to emphasise bending time and space.

Such diegetic sound (what the characters can hear) is used self-consciously and parodically to great effect in the film as a whole. As Neo awakes to the sound of his alarm after meeting Trinity at a club, the sound is the link between the two scenes – not only waking Neo up, but working with the visual as an editing bridge (sound is an important element of editing). The squeaks of the window washers that punctuate Neo's managerial telling off first magnify (quite comically) the grid-based linearity of the world of the matrix, but secondly draw attention to (a) what Neo will later be asked to climb onto to escape the Agents and (b) that he may be being watched.

When Neo arrives to meet Morpheus for the first time, thunder sounds (and lightning flashes) through the rain and periodically sounds during pivotal moments in the scene – seeing Morpheus for the first time and Neo taking the red pill for example. The irony is, of course, that none of this thunder is 'real', allowing for a playful, knowing parody of the filmic convention of using dramatic weather to create mood and tension.

The musical score of *The Matrix* has two main components – orchestral and popular music. Both showcase and enhance the thematic and spectacular power of the film, appealing to young audiences with the contemporary hip hop and dance tracks but also using classical scoring with both sophistication and innovation, incorporating the generic melting pot of references within the film. It is worth noting that the music in the film works extremely well as editing bridge to form sharp cuts that maintain the edge and pace.

As mentioned, orchestral scoring within science fiction creates an organic sound that works well in contrast to the electronic effects and music. In *The Matrix* the orchestral score works to emphasise the human elements of the narrative, with the electronic sounds ascribed to the digital matrix codes and the machines. For the most part the score involves muted and non-muted brass (used often for dramatic moments), strings (for emotional and/or ominous implications) and choral music. It is subtle where needed (at times a barely noticeable backdrop) and foregrounded where appropriate – meaning it is neither a crutch for emotional impact nor mere high-impact sensory noise for the 'big' moments. The majority of the orchestral score is in a minor key, which automatically sounds more unsettling. Staccato (short, sharp notes) is used very heavily during times of high tension as are discordant and more conventional chords during particular moments of action. Also important is the use of silence and muffled sound, such as when Neo is shot by Smith near the end of the film. The sound of a gun firing at point blank would be deafening. This muffling heightens the impact of what has happened – the hero has been killed.

The choral music is very important. It is the most human and organic of musical sounds, coming purely from multiple human voices, and has religious connotations. It is used only at key moments of either birth or rebirth – Neo waking in his 'tank' and seeing the towering human power farm (overlaid with the harsh electric/static sounds of the machines), as he is airlifted from the water, and most dramatically, used at the end as Neo is resurrected and sees the matrix in code for the first time. This is the only time in the film when the music turns to a major key (a 'happier' key), symbolising a huge breakthrough both for the character the film and the audience – it is a moment of exaltation and the choir and brass section are centre stage. Choral music's explicit religious references ties in with Neo as saviour figure as it is used most prominently at Neo's rebirth and resurrection.

A more subtle and playful use of classical music is the scene where we learn of Cypher's betrayal. The scene opens with a harp playing – seeming almost heavenly/angelic but also working alongside Cypher's desire for an epicurean existence contrasting such bourgeois frills as an excellent steak dinner with the utilitarianism of the 'real' world. He will betray/kill his friends for thirty pieces of silver, in other words.

A combination of both contemporary and classical sounds seamlessly enhances the **kung fu/dojo fight** scene between Neo and Morpheus. At the start, in keeping with the classically oriental setting, oriental-style gongs and drums accompany the 'whooshes' of their fight moves. After a pause they begin fighting again, this time accompanied by a pulsating dance track which stops and starts according to the fight's status, ending exactly when the fight is over.

Another key action scene which similarly employs a blend of orchestral and dance music alongside prominent sound effects is the spectacular **lobby scene**. Working with editing, metallic-sounding chords start as Morpheus is under interrogation from Smith, getting louder and louder until Neo's feet (in combat boots) appear through the doors. When the troops have arrived (accompanied by military drums on the soundtrack), the way is paved for a perfectly synchronised action set-piece starting with a well-chosen dance track ('Spybreak' by The Propellerheads) to create an overwhelming sense of 'cool'. The level of noise of the scene – the gunfire of automatics as well as shotguns – is also played with, and the slow motion moments have the sound of slow motion bullets being fired. Exploding pillars, a softer, less violent sound, accompany the sublime visual effects. As the fight ends with a final in-the-air kick from Neo, so too the music track does, leaving only the crisp sound of a gun hitting the floor and Neo and Trinity silently (and humorously) leaving the lobby. That the entire scene, cartwheels, gunfights, gun throwing, etc. is choreographed so successfully demonstrates the benefit of the fusion of music and sound with action to enhance pace and heighten sensory impact to create a ballet of bullets. The scene as an action set-piece also bears hallmarks of a music video in its reliance on music and choreography.

Scenes where popular music enhances the 'cool' factor include the 'woman in the red dress' scene where Rob D's 'Clubbed to Death' track pulsates upwards in a foreboding, minor key as Neo and Morpheus walk against the crowd; the track playing as the group go into the matrix to see the Oracle (the camera pans round them in each 'world' whilst a phone rings as a beat moves the action along;) and the aptly-named end title track 'Wake Up' by Rage Against the Machine, again edited to form a deftly executed finale.

Use of Camera

The innovative use of camera overall is a definitive feature of *The Matrix*. Having looked at 'bullet time' it is still important to examine briefly the film's formal use of camera and editing. The film blends 450 special effect shots with a range of camerawork suitable for differentiating the 'real' world from that within the matrix. Within the real world, long lenses emphasise the characters as opposed to the backgrounds whereas within the matrix it is the backgrounds themselves, as well as the characters' interaction with them, that are highlighted.

Particularly key shots used at various points in the film are **low and high angles**. The low angle shots (when the camera is placed low to the ground looking up) tend to be used to create a sense of majesty and enormity, whilst high angle shots (the camera looking down) particularly on characters and their situations can make them appear vulnerable. *The Matrix* uses a combination of both. For example, when Neo is taken to meet Morpheus for the first time we see an extreme high angle shot looking down from the tall building at the small characters below as rain pours down (a shot reminiscent of *Blade Runner*). We then look up at the same building from the characters point of view, the combination of both offering insights into the idea that characters are being watched and also that Neo is nervous – all achieved using low and high angle shot-reverse-shots.

Again, when we see the helicopter pass over the building where Morpheus is captive it is in extreme low angle, expertly framed in high contrast with glass skyscrapers offering mirror images of the black helicopter (there are several low angle shots of the helicopter and its blades, making full use of the shapes both create with the machine as a pitch black silhouette). High angles are also used to offer us Neo's point of view – when he is climbing out onto the ledge of the skyscraper to evade the Agents we see his view dozens of storeys up (this fear must then be conquered by him literally jumping from a skyscraper in the 'jump programme').

Neo's role as central protagonist is emphasised by many **point of view (POV) shots**, this *mode of address* cleverly putting the audience very much in his position allowing for empathy and recognition. As the narrative unravels, we the audience learn only when Neo does of the true nature of his reality, making him our point of identification increased by the use of the camera. A particularly good example of this is Neo's awakening in his tank of amniotic slime. As he does so the camera is placed to see what he sees (and be as baffled as he is), and after seeing the towers of humans in similar states as he is flushed down a series of tubes, again the camera/audience is seeing what Neo sees (going down the 'ride' as well, tumbling down the rabbit hole). In the 'real' world as he opens his eyes for the first time so too does the camera and so on. In contrast Morpheus is often shot from behind – in the lift and the car going to see the Oracle – which is again Neo's point of view further placing the audience alongside Neo, with Morpheus still an enigma.

Not only does the use of POV shots increase identification it also places the viewer very much in the thick of the action – as Neo grabs onto the harness to hold Trinity from the helicopter and is pulled towards the edge of the roof, the viewer is also pulled fast by the POV camera angle – our sense of urgency, exhilaration and participation is increased. Similarly during Neo's final chase sequence the camera is hand-held and jerky, reminiscent of another Reeves film, *Point Break* (1991), ahead of him then behind him, running into the apartment where *The Prisoner* is playing on the television. When he is shot suddenly by Smith on entering Room 303 near the end (the same room Trinity is caught in at the beginning, its number referring to Christianity), we see his hands touch the blood from the bullet hole as if we are Neo looking down in slow motion (enhanced by the muffled sound and instantaneous flash from the gun). In the final vindication of his powers following his 'resurrection', as he sees *the matrix* in code for the first time, so does the viewer.

Close ups in *the matrix* itself tend to frame the characters either side of the frame with their shoulders in full view, working with costume to create the desired effect. During dialogue sequences there are many shot-reverse-shots.

Tracking shots (where the camera is placed on a track and moved alongside a character) are used in the lobby sequence as Neo runs between the pillars. During the lobby scene it is used in combination with **slow motion**, another prominent camera technique within the film. Most visible in the lobby sequence (Neo and Trinity's slo-mo cartwheels are sublimely choreographed), the technique is used regularly within *the matrix* to maximise the impact of the stunts, the manipulation of time and complementing the bullet time sequences. Noticeable slow motion sequences include the dojo/kung fu fight, Morpheus escaping his captors, Neo grabbing the helicopter harness and, most dramatically, at the climax of Neo's race to Room 303 and his subsequent shooting.

The Wachowskis often use the camera as self-consciously as other elements. The lobby scene interestingly also begins with a tilt up from Neo's combat boots to his face, making him seem powerful. The beginning of the showdown between Neo and Smith has cameras placed next to each character's hips – instantly recognisable as the tension-building pistol holster shot of many a western gunfight (with paper blowing across the set reminiscent of tumble weed). **Editing** is often similarly stylised, with flashlights at the beginning in keeping with the references to film noir and Neo's matrix experiences (his 'dreams' and 'waking up' to his alarm clock, etc.) swiftly moving from scene

Neo hides behind a pillar in the lobby sequence

to scene. Thematic concerns of images and reality (simulation and simulacra) are highlighted with the camera moving impossibly though screens (e.g. the digits at the opening, through the monitor watching Neo and into the interrogation room, and out of the television set Morpheus has used to show Neo the 'real' world). This is in contrast to Hollywood's tendency for continuity editing, which uses editing to conceal rather than reveal the film as construct. The Wachowskis want us to revel in the stylisation and artifice of *The Matrix* as well as engage with it. This mainstream appropriation of stylistic foregrounding of film as construct (by rendering its component parts visible and emphasised, as was the intention of the German Expressionism movement of the 1920s) is often associated with independent and art cinema, whose concerns have been with the nature of film itself. That *The Matrix* manages to engage with this aesthetic as well as the pervasive MTV-style cinematic trend for choreographed visual pleasure further demonstrates the variety of the film's different elements.

24 & 25 Scarratt, ibid, 2001
26 Scarratt, ibid, 2001
27 Jacobs, 'Gunfire', in Action/Spectacle Cinema, 2000
28 The Wachowskis' Interview, www.whatisthematrix.com
29 www.whatisthematrix.com
30 Street, *The Matrix*, Fashioning the Future in Costume and Cinema, 2001
31 Street, ibid, 2001
32 *The Matrix* Revisited DVD, 2001
33 *The Matrix* Revisited DVD, 2001
34 *The Matrix* DVD, 1999
35 *The Matrix* Revisited DVD, 2001

5. Characterisation / Representation

Names

In keeping with the comic book elements of the film, the names of the characters are often almost a short-hand potted character description. This semantic technique was used in the Wachowskis first film, Bound, to denote character differences – Violet (feminine, glamorous and sometimes vulnerable), Corky (sexy, sassy, leather-clad, truck-driving) and Caesar (ruthless, scheming). This literal use of language combines with other elements (including costume, lighting and colour among others) to form instant signifiers that tap into existing meanings (often cultural or visual but in the case of words, actual/literal).

The Matrix continues this style. **Matrix** originally meant 'womb', its latter meanings relating to the place where things are formed and in mathematical terms the columns and rows of numerology. That both meanings apply to the themes of the film, that of human entrapment in womb-like pods and the mathematical computer generated world which similarly entraps them is a dual play on words. So is the **Nebuchadnezzar** – the rebel's ship in the real world. Nebuchadnezzar was the King of Babylon who defeated the Egyptians, captured Jerusalem and restored Babylon to its former glory. Written about in the Book of Daniel he is also the King who has a dream that he cannot remember but strives to – similar to Neo's quest aboard the 'Neb'. On the metal core of the craft is written 'Mark III No.11', visible only briefly as Morpheus introduces Neo to the ship and crew. The Book of Mark states 'And whenever unclean spirits beheld him, they fell down before him and cried out "You are the Son of God"'.[36] The last remaining human city, the final frontier as it were, is **Zion**. Again connoting religious meaning, the word was originally another name for Jerusalem in the Old Testament, and the place where God dwells and reigns with the faithful (heaven).

Within the film itself there is also much play on **numbers** as well as words, particularly in terms of locations. The digits at the beginning of the film are **555**, numerology that relates to the Messiah (555 is also the default Hollywood fake area code used to prevent keen-eyed viewers dialling actual numbers).[37] The room where Trinity is ambushed is number **303**, the same room where Neo is shot by Agent Smith at the end, where Trinity revives him while he lies dead outside it. Trinity as a word has heavy connotations of the number 3. Thomas Anderson/Neo's apartment is visibly number **101** as he opens the door to his client, a reference to George Orwell's 1984, Room 101 being that which contains one's worst fears.

The use of names of characters has even more meaning. **Neo** is an anagram of 'one'. He is continuously referred to in the film as 'the One', the saviour of humanity, who will bring about the destruction of *the matrix*. Who will, in other words, introduce a new order – neo, meaning 'new'. That he has two names/two lives at the beginning and is also the ordinary everyman Thomas Anderson, highlights the fact that he must choose an identity, and by the name connotations, must choose either to be special or be 'just another guy'. That Agent Smith continuously calls him 'Mr Anderson' is indicative of his refusal to acknowledge Neo's power or 'true' identity. Anderson comes from the Greek andre, meaning 'man', so Anderson means 'son of man', a phrase used by Jesus. Similarly his first name could derive from the 'Doubting Thomas' disciple 'who expresses scepticism about accounts that Jesus had risen from the dead'[38] – Neo's continuous self-doubts are his hindrances. 'Doubting Thomas' would only believe in the resurrection if he placed his fingers into the spear wound on Christ's side, portrayed in famous paintings using two fingers. Neo places two fingers into the mirror of *the matrix* after taking the red pill, his first step towards knowing the 'truth' and combating self-doubt.

In terms of names and dialogue it is also noticeable that many of the characters say 'Jesus' or 'Jesus Christ' either to, or referring to, Neo. From his client, who calls him his 'saviour' and 'own personal Jesus Christ' (and then goes on to say that if asked, Neo doesn't exist) to the numerous times the traitorous Cypher uses the phrase. Whilst at first this may seem only a standard use of blasphemy/swearing as an expression of emotion, that it relates specifically to this 'saviour' is arguably positioning Neo as a similar figure, predicted by the Oracle as some religious groups predict a 'second coming'. And the words are used only in relation to Neo. As well as being reborn and resurrected he is also in a sense a virgin birth, having never been born from humans, another deliberate religious reference.

Morpheus, as mentor, commander of the ship, leader of the resistance, as the person who instructs Neo in the ways of *the matrix*, is defined as the 'God of dreams', the word meaning literally 'he who forms' – again an appropriate name for the person who wakes Neo from his slumber to show him that he has 'been living in a dream world' in order to transform him into 'the One'. His resistance fighters can manipulate and use *the matrix* to fight against it and in this sense he is a powerful figure, but not the one who can change it (if he is God, as it were, Neo is Jesus).

Trinity again alludes to religious imagery as well as strong connotations of the number three. It is assumed to be her 'hacker' name in the same way that prior to his induction into the real world 'Neo' is Thomas Anderson's hacker alias.

In a sense she makes the third of a party of three alongside Morpheus and Neo (the 'trinity' of Father, Son and Holy Ghost?) – it is the power of her love which can save/resurrect Neo and also help him in numerous situations throughout the film.

Cypher is the treacherous, Judas character who chooses the matrix over the 'real' world, on the basis that 'ignorance is bliss'. His position is not that hard to appreciate given the hardships the rebels endure in this real world; however he is made abominable by his callous killing of almost all the ship's crew and his betrayal of Morpheus. His name has multiple meanings – 'secret writing' (he meets Agent Smith secretly within *the matrix*, which is written in code), and also comes from the Arabic word for 'zero', or 'a person of no importance'. It is potentially feelings of the latter (in comparison to Neo or Morpheus he is not important, neither special nor object of Trinity's love) which lead him to be of *considerable* importance through his act of betrayal. Some have also noticed the likely joke-reference made when Cypher meets Agent Smith over a 'juicy and delicious' steak in *the matrix*. Smith refers to him as 'Mr Reagan' (presumably meant to be Cyper's surname), and Cypher indicates he would like to 'remember nothing' and 'be someone important…like an actor'. Whether indeed this is a jibe at the memory-impaired former American president or not has not been clarified but it would seem a little in-joke also about the elevated status afforded to actors in our world.

The remainder of the crew carry names with varying degrees of metaphorical meaning – **Tank**, **Dozer** (brothers, both of colour, the latter possibly short for bulldozer due to his size), **Mouse** (perhaps a reference to *Alice in Wonderland*), Apoc (short for apocalypse) and most tellingly, **Switch**. The only other female member of the crew, she is also the only blonde, and at one point in *the matrix* wears all white – the absolute opposite of the dark look of the others, which along with her hair gives her an almost albino look – a complete switch, in other words, from the rest. **The Oracle** (it is a title rather than a name) is one who prophesises and predicts the future. That she should be a homely lady in a kitchen making cookies is another reference to mythology. In ancient Greece the Delphic Oracle was a woman who gave honey and barley cakes to those who asked her advice.

Agent Smith's name is also a play on words – such Agents 'are everyone, and they are no one'. Smith is a common surname (often cited as the most common) emphasising this element of their nature – that the programme can become anyone at anytime. It might also be noted that the hero of *1984* is named Winston Smith. In *Matrix Reloaded* and *Matrix Revolutions* this name/character description trend continues with a range of new identities and meanings (as discussed in the section on *The Matrix Reloaded*).

Neo/Thomas Anderson

Much has been written on the action genre's preoccupation with male protagonists and their representation of particular types of masculinity and 'musculinity', the term given by Yvonne Tasker (1998) to describe the body-building heroes of the 80s and early 90s. *The Matrix*, as a part action movie, seemingly conforms to the notion of a male hero in the character of Neo. Laura Mulvey's seminal essay 'Visual Pleasure and Narrative Cinema' (1975) states clearly that in terms of spectatorship, the man on screen is the *point of identification*, not the *object of desire* – that is reserved for the female, thus making her the passive object of both the on screen male's active look and that of the audience. These assertions now seem oversimplified; McDonald argues 'spectatorship is far more complex than the easy association

Neo / Thomas Anderson

of male or female spectators with masculine or feminine positions',[39] which allows for more fluid interpretations of gender representations and characteristics on film, as well as the audience's engagement with the film text.

This 'cross-gender identification' is well demonstrated by *The Matrix* – the audience, not knowing what *the matrix* is, identifies with Neo, who is in a similar position. This works at both the level of identification and also endears the audience to Neo as his world is turned upside down. In this sense the use of Keanu Reeves (a sex symbol) offers visual pleasure as 'audiences can delight in the litheness of Reeves' body, fighting and reactions'[40] – the characters of both Neo and Trinity can both be interpreted as objects of desire as well as a progressive action hero and heroine.

At the start of the film, the character of Thomas Anderson/ Neo is not very spectacular at all. First shown as an illegal hacker, he is alone in his early scenes (and this can be read as isolated) – alone in his apartment until first his computer and then his clients contact him (both coming from the resistance), alone in the club where Trinity approaches him (he is passively waiting), and alone in his empty, colourless work cubicle. His 'legitimate' life is a cover for his life as a computer hacker, which at least partially explains his isolation. That he is a hacker lends him coolness – character types in science fiction tend to polarise between computer-literate characters as 'geeks' or more risky 'hackers'. This competence in computer programmes (and the fact that he is in fact living inside one) places him outside society already, allying him with the resistance. However he is not an action hero at this point – when told by Morpheus to use a scaffold to escape to the roof of a skyscraper, he tries and fails, and is instead captured by the agents. Once captured, however, he does display a stubborn belief in his rights (giving the agents 'the finger' and insisting on his phone call) that demonstrates a certain irreverence.

He is referred to as *Alice In Wonderland* on more than one occasion – moments before Neo and the audience discover the truth about *the matrix*, Morpheus says he imagines Neo feels 'a bit like Alice', then pauses to say 'tumbling down the rabbit-hole'. This pause is just long enough to show a perplexed Neo (mirroring the audience), in effect being likened to a female, then allowing the equating of a male hero with a young girl from children's fiction to register. It is an image which disrupts preconceptions of masculinity, but it also does aptly describe how he must be feeling if one knows the story of *Alice in Wonderland*. It also refers to the cryptic 'follow the white rabbit' motif that has already been used – which, once we know what they know, seems apt indeed.

As a character he could be likened to the Luke Skywalker of the first *Star Wars* film – a young man on the brink of maturity who does not yet know his own importance or have the confidence or self-belief necessary to reveal his true potential. Anakin in *Star Wars Episode I: The Phantom Menace* is referred to as 'the One who will bring balance to the Force'. Neo, however, must go further – he must be 'reborn' before he can find his true 'fate'. This rebirth sequence is how both Neo, and the audience, have the 'real' world revealed to them. Neo wakes up in a sack of fluid, naked and connected to machines through invasive black cables (comparable to the umbilical cord) that are then painfully expelled from him as he is thrown down a waste disposal shaft and left to drown (presumably unable to swim as he has never used his muscles) until he is rescued – brought up to the light, literally, as he is hoisted up to the hovercraft. This birth image gives the hero a vulnerability – his nakedness, his unawareness of the 'real' world, lack of hair and eyebrows, all equate with the birth of an infant and, having never been really born at all but manufactured and farmed by the computers, it could be argued that this is in fact his actual (virgin) birth, with his later resurrection leading to his *rebirth* as 'the One'.

Once aboard the craft he is subjected to being 'rebuilt' – his muscles are built up using needles, his black bolts are removed. All of these images show a defenceless hero through this focus on his naked body being entrusted to strangers. That his body is displayed is not a new phenomenon in the action genre; it is the way it is displayed that is important, since it exposes Neo's vulnerability that is later concealed by the costumes he wears when he is in *the matrix*.[41] It is a far cry from the 'musculinity' of the 80s action genre's 'hard men' where masculinity is fixed and deliberately/reassuringly impenetrable.

Further, that Neo is also 'rescued' would appear to link him with the more traditionally feminine role – and this has ramifications for the representation of Trinity in terms of her appropriation of some 'masculine' characteristics (both characters are fully versed in martial arts and weaponry). Cypher at one point refers to Neo's 'big, pretty eyes' – something more commonly used to describe women, but also an image of doe-eyed innocence. Even The Oracle comically says he's 'not too bright though', and in this sense Neo knows less than those around him, but all this will change as he moves towards being 'the One' so that by the end he can overcome even death. This age-old notion of innocence to experience is what transforms him into fully-fledged Messiah figure but also action hero for the next two films. In this sense his is 'born' twice – first, his birth awakening out of his matrix-slumber, the other his resurrection and rebirth, after death, as 'the One'. His powers are only truly and unequivocally realised after his 'death'. As the Oracle predicted, either Morpheus or Neo would die – Neo does – but she also predicted he was 'waiting for something ... maybe your next life'. One aids the other, death to life as it were, another allegorical reference to a Christ-like figure.

The use of stars in films has also been discussed in terms of their meaning generically and culturally as well as their potentially disruptive impact on a film's narrative – with Classical Hollywood narrative the emphasis on making the film as 'real' as possible is undercut by the presence of a star and its external meanings. Certain stars are often associated with specific genres and are 'signs' to audiences connoting a familiar reference. As a star, Keanu Reeves has been around for some time. He garnered critical praise for his first performance of note in *River's Edge* (1986) as a troubled teenager. However his first box office success was as the goofy, loveably dim Ted 'Theodore' Logan in *Bill and Ted's Excellent Adventure* (1989), a role he reprised in *Bill and Ted's Bogus Journey* (1991) and which, bizarrely, also had him and his friend as the saviours of society. He played similar low-key roles in *Parenthood* (1989) and *I Love You To Death* (1990), but punctuated such performances with serious dramas from *Dangerous Liasons* (1989) to independent fare like Gus Van Sant's *My Own Private Idaho*, 1991 (in which he boldly plays a street hustler), *Much Ado About Nothing* (1993), and *The Devil's Advocate* (1997).

Possibly because of his early 'goofball' roles, possibly also because of his status as a sex symbol for women, Reeves has rarely enjoyed critical acclaim for his actual *acting*. Despite this he has starred in over 30 films that have in total earned over a billion dollars worth of box office revenue,[42] with the *average* take of his last ten films being over $40m in the USA alone. As a star he seems private, with reports of him giving some of his acting fees to other cast and crew members. His fee for *The Matrix* was $10m, and for the two sequels he will earn $15m for each film, indicating his star power and his perceived importance to the success of the first film. It was also reported that the actor waived an agreed percentage of the revenue for the two sequels in order to prevent jeopardising their production.

Reeves' diverse career and roles indicates one thing in particular – he is not a star associated with any one particular genre. His three most similar roles to *The Matrix* are arguably in the action thriller *Point Break* (Kathryn Bigelow's adrenaline/stunt-fuelled, surfing-based 'wet western'), the commercially disappointing William Gibson adaptation *Johnny Mnemonic* and his second most successful film, *Speed* (1994). The latter catapulted him into superstardom as an action hero of the new order– one who was slender, sexy and more gung-ho by far than Neo. It is perhaps partly because of *Speed*, perhaps partially due to the actor's lack of overt self-promotion that Reeves was a suitably blank canvas for the part of Neo – surprise is expressed even now at the 'risk taken in casting Keanu Reeves as the man on the spot'.[43] Although a star with continuous box office appeal, his star persona does not appear to disrupt the narrative. Much of his acting in *The Matrix* involves *reacting* (not in itself uncommon for an action-orientated film) – he, like the audience, has no idea what is happening for the first part of the film and must listen whilst he learns from his tutor/mentor, Morpheus. In the years following the success of *The Matrix* he has taken on riskier roles – of serial killer in *The Watcher* (2000) and wife-beater in *The Gift* (2000).

Trinity

One review of *The Matrix* states that 'Trinity is simply the latest in a long series of "action women" to be found in contemporary Hollywood'.[44] This statement totally disregards ways in which Trinity is an extremely interesting point of study in terms of representation. The 'action women' title was coined from the emergence of the first (Ripley in the *Alien* series) and continued to analyse similar roles from a feminist perspective. Sarah Connor in *Terminator 2* became a progressive display of cross-gender identification as well as a character with multiple masculine/feminine characteristics. Such women in the action/sci fi genres have often been given freedom from the traditional gender boundaries associated with classical Hollywood cinema. Often 'the displaced settings encourage subversion of typical roles and representations'[45]

Trinity

– a factor that can be applied to both Trinity and Neo.

Similarly to Neo as 'new' action hero, Trinity too is sleeker and less overtly muscular than, for example, Linda Hamilton in *T2*. Also, unlike Sarah Connor in *The Terminator*, Trinity is not transformed through the narrative. Whilst both the males in that film – Kyle Connor and *The Terminator*

– are fully aware and trained for all eventualities, Sarah Connor's journey is from a woman 'who can't even balance her chequebook' to fully fledged action heroine (a learning curve similar to Neo's). She has been inducted into the 'real world' and is a competent woman able to handle herself. Trinity represents an unusual and seemingly progressive action heroine. She does not abide by the rules Tasker identifies in the female sidekick to an action hero – she is neither an affirmation of the hero's heterosexuality nor a victim to provide the hero's character motivation, but a distinctive and highly competent character in her own right. However she does incorporate elements of both – she is indeed the love interest, and in saving her from the helicopter Neo does at least partially discover his power. So these definitions are not without complication and contradiction, particularly as the film progresses. It is also important to bear in mind that alongside her status as action heroine in Hollywood cinema, Trinity also bears elements of the female martial arts heroine. Very popular in the 1970s in Hong Kong cinema, such roles have recently been imitated in mainstream films.

At the opening, however, it is extremely important that it is Trinity we see first as the active character. As she sits in a dark, noirish building, outside a policeman makes a dismissive remark – 'I think we can handle one little girl' – that is then contradicted by Agent Smith, leading to tension as we wait to see how this woman will respond to the encroaching police units. Our first view of her face as the camera tilts up from behind her laptop makes her look pale under the flashlights and also in contrast to her slicked back hair and dark background. What happens next has been parodied, copied and stolen multiple times yet nothing quite prepares one for the first viewing as Trinity leaps into the air, defying time and gravity as the camera then moves right around her ('bullet time' photography) following which she overwhelms a room full of policemen. Unsure whether she is a 'good' character, a criminal or even an alien at this point, we then witness her performing other unfeasible stunts as she escapes the agent who pursues her.

As previously stated, Trinity's costumes within the artificial matrix are self-consciously tight, figure hugging and verging on fetishistic in their extensive use of constricting PVC. This first stunt, however, indicates a further use for her costumes – that they reflect the light, highlighting her silhouette and movement and therefore adding greatly to the impact and spectacle of the action sequence. Yes, a figure-hugging catsuit has been used before – from Catwoman to *Barb Wire* (1996) or to more progressive effect in *Strange Days* – but seldom to such spectacular effect. Added to this is the concept that Trinity is *active*, complicating her relationship to the male gaze and, as with Neo, allowing for cross-gender identification as well as simultaneous objectification. Similarly she does not resemble the exaggeratedly sexual, busty heroines of the comic book (or even the unfeasibly curvaceous Lara Croft) but in the form of actress Carrie-Anne Moss is personified as an androgynous heroine who, like Reeves, is sexy with cross-gender characteristics. She wears minimal make up, has her hair slicked back and, as with the other characters, is the epitome of 'coolness' in her black outfits with designer shades – all contributing to the look of the film and its powerful appeal. They also play with the conventions of gender boundaries by using fashion as a tool of androgyny and diversity in femininity/masculinity.

However, arguably her identity and role become far more feminine and traditional in the real world, where she wears the same grey costumes as everyone else but has feminine hair, takes Neo his food and serves under the hierarchical leadership of Morpheus. This raises questions about whether there is more room for progressiveness in *the matrix* than in the real world, which rather undermines the film's thematic critique of postmodernism. The irony is that Trinity seems freer, more of an action heroine, within the artificial world.

Once again, however, this is potentially an over-simplification and the key lies in the relationship between Trinity and Neo. As Neo meets her for the first time, he shows surprise. His knowledge of Trinity as a computer hacker is disrupted as he states 'I always thought you were a guy'. Trinity's clear competence with technology, guns and even at one point a helicopter are all 'symbolically transgressive iconography'[46] allowing her to meet the male hero on mutual ground. More important than this, however, in disrupting Trinity's more traditional presentation in the real world, is the exchange that occurs as Neo attempts to rescue Morpheus alone. Trinity insists she goes with him, pulling rank and telling him to literally 'go to hell' if he doesn't like it. The relationship between Trinity and Neo is more of a partnership than anything else, in which, at least initially Trinity has more power. She not only rescues him from the matrix itself, Neo actually asks for her help as he confronts an agent on the rooftop and is about to be shot. She comes to his aid holding a gun point blank at an agent ('Dodge this').

It is pivotal to Neo both that he saves Trinity from the helicopter but also that she must be removed from the arena in order for him to fully realise his potential. This is done deftly as Trinity is transported back into the matrix moments before an agent shoots the phone therefore cutting Neo off and leaving him alone. This is Neo's time, as it were, to be showcased in an action sequence in the matrix itself, but there is a feeling that both have been allowed individual action sequences as well as ones as partners. If it appears that Neo is surpassing her, it is her declaration of love for him that literally resurrects him as he lies dead. This does then lead to him becoming 'the One' and therefore they are no longer of equal importance. Trinity's powers diminish and her role becomes one of loving female to release the hero's true potential. However as science fiction traditionally has less room for romance, with it being thematically often functional to the narrative, here the final kiss (Neo's first 'real' one) is a tender moment that successfully avoids demonstrating the lovers' difference, but rather connects them on different terms. This sudden display of emotion sits slightly uneasily next to Trinity's warrior-like status within the matrix, but it does relate to the threefold Christian power of her name, signifying 'the ideology that the spirit within humans is the most powerful force in the universe'.[47] This also relates to the modernist sensibilities presented by the 'real' world of the film and which relegates the stylish costumes of the matrix as mere window dressing to the 'true' powers that humans possess.

The Matrix put model-turned-actress Carrie-Anne Moss into the big league and established her as a star. Whether Trinity's character would have had such an impact had she been played by an existing major star (bringing with her the distractions of external references) is an interesting question and brings to the fore issues of stardom in relation to narrative and characterisation There is no real pre-conception therefore from Moss's previous roles and this further enhances her believability as the character. Worth noting also is the presentations of femininity offered by the Wachowskis in their previous film, *Bound*, and how Trinity arguably sprang at least in part from these.

Morpheus

Morpheus

The character of Morpheus is that of mentor. If *The Matrix* toys with issues of gender representation it also deals with the representation of race. Several characters of colour are presented – Morpheus, Tank, Dozer and Apoc (the first three being African-Americans and the latter appearing to be of either Maori or Polynesian origin), all are part of the resistance. Richard Dyer (writing coincidentally about another Reeves film, Speed, as action film) states: 'We now have a well-established pattern whereby the hero is accompanied by white women and men of colour (rarely women of colour) who are also exposed to the dangers that bring the thrills'.[48] The sentence indicates the ongoing dominance of the white male hero still in the action genre (although there have been recent successful examples of black hero figures such as Will Smith and Wesley Snipes), and the concession that is the inclusion of women and men of colour as subordinate characters.

This could be said of *The Matrix*, in that Neo is still the main point of identification for the audience. However in the hierarchy of the film and the 'real' world, Morpheus is the most powerful character. Neo's power as 'the One' to manipulate *the matrix* will be to serve Morpheus's purpose as leader of the resistance. To see Morpheus and Trinity as 'concessionary', to disrupt the dominance of the white male hero, is dismissive of their progressive roles within the film. It could further be read that the leader of the resistance is black, and that the agents are white, embodying power struggles and critiquing the world of *the matrix* (i.e. that most similar to ours).

As with Trinity, when first encountered, the audience (again identifying with Neo) is unsure how to perceive Morpheus. He is described by Agent Smith, who we are also unsure of as he conforms to our preconceived ideological notions of a powerful law/government representative, as a 'known terrorist'. Image, signs and assumptions of reality and meaning are being played with. When first introduced, it is by voice over a mobile phone – Morpheus's verbal gravitas is a powerful element as he will be the one to explain *the matrix* to us and to Neo, as well as be the voice of the philosophy at the film's centre.

When Neo first meets him in person, he is presented self-consciously styled – standing upright in a long leather coat, with thunder and lightning punctuating the scene at key moments. Morpheus has his back to both Neo and the camera and as he turns, smiling, his mirror-lensed shades render him inscrutable. His shades lack arms – another differentiating factor and promotion of his uniqueness.

As a character Morpheus is a leader of his crew (and of the resistance) and therefore a man of power. He is mentor to Neo, and is pivotal to the key elements of the film's plotting – it is he who believes Neo is 'the One', he who articulates this, and it is, most importantly, he who explains what *the matrix* is to both Neo and the audience. This enhances his power over both. At first his cryptic statements enhance his mystique. Then as he becomes more involved in Neo's training we enjoy watching them spar in the kung fu fighting programme, witnessing the power of Morpheus both physically and in his command of Zen-like wisdom. To save Neo he demonstrates enormous mind over matter at various points (by breaking through a wall, fighting an agent and breaking apart handcuffs). That he must be taken and beaten by multiple policemen with truncheons inevitably brings to mind police beatings such as that of Rodney King and also emphasises his enormous power as leader of a social movement attempting to instigate change, as did the Civil Rights movement of the 1960s. If he is the God and Master of Dreams, then Neo is his son, as it were, the numerous Jesus Christ references again not just asserting Neo's position but also that of Morpheus as God-like. As a genre that deals with existential questions, science fiction is noted for giving characters dialogue that may be philosophical or contemplative – it is Morpheus in *The Matrix* who can speculate about social consequences of characters' actions. However his musings are in fact vitally important to revealing the film's plot (and subtexts).

Morpheus' costumes break with the jet-blacks worn by the other resistance fighters. His ties are green, his suits brownish, noted by some to be similar colours to those worn by the Agents – perhaps equating him with their level of power. The long leather coat he wears is arguably styled on black heroes such as *Shaft* (1971) as well as looking like crocodile skin (also worn by Cypher), but in the 'real' world Morpheus dresses in similar attire to his crew – unlike in many instances on film, his role as leader is not coded through uniform.

It could be argued that by the end of *The Matrix* Morpheus is in a similar position to Trinity – he will still play a vital role in bringing about change but he has been surpassed in importance by Neo becoming 'the One'. His faith in Neo is what leads us to believe that he must indeed be 'the One' before Neo himself realises this. When he tells Neo he won't have to dodge bullets, this is true – Neo is shot multiple times but resurrects, proving Morpheus right. In the 'real' world, however, as previously stated, Morpheus's importance is that of leader. He will still guide Neo (and the next two sequels) as spiritual leader, speaker of truth and bearer of knowledge.

In terms of stardom, Laurence Fishburne is again not an actor associated with the science fiction genre specifically. Fishburne is a recognisably powerful and 'heavyweight' performer having starred in many films from *Othello* (1995), *Boyz N the Hood* (1991) and *What's Love Got to Do With It?* (1993) as well as featuring in *Apocalypse Now* (1979), *Rumble Fish* (1983) and *King of New York* (1990). His qualities – of commanding respect and wielding power (both physical and verbal) – are vital to the role of Morpheus. An irony, considering their on screen roles, is that he is only actually three years older than Keanu Reeves.

Agent Smith

Smith is the human face of the machines – a recognisable form of an enemy not of our species. He is the villain. That he, and the other two agents, dress like Secret Service agents uses pre-existing ideological iconography to imply 'the Agents are the true holders of power'.[49] This is at least partially achieved by comparative dress and again pre-existing notions of power struggles. For instance at the opening of the film we see law enforcement officers (dressed in cop uniforms) arrive to capture Trinity. When the agents arrive, headed by Smith, their costume of suits, ties (each with matching tie pins), sunglasses and ear pieces instantly elevates their status to that of, at the very least, FBI agents, the superiors of these run-of-the-mill policemen. 'On a political level, this contrast relates to conflict between federal and local power structures. The rebels thus represent a challenge to and resentment of federal authority'.[50]

That the colours of their outfits match the sepia shades of *the matrix* (always tinted green) shows their direct relationship to that system, as the 'unseen' powers beyond the police. That their powers extend vastly beyond that again brings to mind the 'government spooks' (e.g. the CIA) who can withhold information and retain absolute but invisible power over the public domain. That they are all white males could be interpreted as a representation of the dominance of the white male in federal/government structures and patriarchal society and again rendering opposed their desire to maintain ideological status quo and that of the multi-racial resistance.

As a figure, Smith is to be feared. Morpheus informs Neo that everyone who has stood their ground and fought an Agent rather than fleeing has died. That they can become anyone at any time means they are, in effect, everywhere. This is demonstrated strikingly in the sequence involving the woman in the red dress who transforms into Smith holding a gun. Within *the matrix* Smith fights both Morpheus and Neo, initially beating both, overcoming Morpheus with armed police

Agent Smith

and thrusting Neo onto a train track; but ultimately being overcome first by Morpheus's refusal to succumb to the drugs they administer and secondly through Neo's first 'killing' of him under a subway train and final dramatic destruction of Smith by jumping inside him. As with many filmic/narrative conventions, an especially nasty death must be sought for the ultimate enemy to offer satisfaction to an audience. Smith must actually be destroyed (only to reappear in the sequels).

He is given further 'personalisation' by his emotive desires to get out of the matrix himself. He isn't just serving it, he hates it, contemptuous of the 'fake' humanity they have created that lacks perfection because it must seem human enough to believe in. This sets him apart from the other agents, with his hatred for the matrix running in parallel with that of the resistance, just with opposing outcomes; the destruction of the resistance versus the destruction of the matrix. It seems more like a personal vendetta, heightening the tension of artificiality and humanity as well as the strength of Smith as a character.

He is the only character, apart from Morpheus, allowed to philosophise. Their contrasting viewpoints, whilst rendering them polar opposites, equate their levels of power in their different spheres. It potentially also renders Morpheus more powerful as he can enter and leave the matrix whilst Smith cannot enter the real world (only send Sentinel machines), not being real himself, but this power is then balanced out by that fact that Morpheus can be killed inside *the matrix* whilst Smith, up until that point, cannot. When they first meet, as Morpheus sacrifices himself for Neo in a display of strength, Smith recognises him ('The great Morpheus' he mocks) to which Morpheus retorts 'You all look the same to me' – demonstrating the contempt felt from both sides. Whilst Morpheus sees the computers as having enslaved man, Smith views humans as a 'plague', with the computers as the 'cure'. As he goes further to liken the human race to a virus, it is hard not to see that on some levels, Smith's critique of the voracious exploitation of our planet's resources is indeed true of our actual world. It also plays with the concepts of inherently presumed ideology – that we should unquestioningly be on the side of the humans, and once again allows for existential and moral speculation with the film about in this case the nature of man. The voice of Agent Smith is evocative and only semi human, speaking in low, deep tones and with unusual pronunciation and intonation at times. The actor Hugo Weaving has stated that he was trying to get across a 'neutral accent, not robotic but not really human',[51] vaguely based on a 50s TV newsreader, as well as the Wachowski brothers themselves. The monotone expressions of his fellow agents once again set him apart from them as being, paradoxically, more 'human', and therefore conflictingly more dangerous.

Australian actor Hugo Weaving, at the time of the release of *The Matrix*, was best known internationally as one of a trio of drag queens in *The Adventures of Priscilla, Queen of the Desert* (1994) and the voice of Rex in *Babe* (1995). In Australia he had received and been nominated for Australian Film Institute awards but was in a sense an anonymous enough face to embody the veneer of a computer programme in human form – familiar yet alien simultaneously. His calibre as an actor and immersion in the role of Smith may at least partially explain why his role is reprised in *The Matrix Reloaded* despite being destroyed at the end of *The Matrix*. Also key is the fact that by the release of Reloaded his career had also moved up a notch with his role as Elrond in the phenomenally successful *The Lord of the Rings trilogy* (2001–2003). Characteristics of stardom carrying external meaning from film to film come into play when thinking about the inevitable cross-over of audiences for each trilogy/franchise.

36 Bassham, The Religion of *The Matrix* and the Problems of Pluralism, in *The Matrix* and Philosophy, 2002

37 Inside Film magazine, issue 7 1999, p.16

38 Bassham, ibid, 2002

39 McDonald, Star Studies in Hollows and Jankovich, Approaches to Popular Film, 1995

40 Scarratt, ibid, 2001

41 Street, ibid, 2001

42 www.themovietimes.com

43 Newman, Rubber Reality, in Science Fiction/Horror, 2002

44 www.nottingham.ac.uk/ film/journal/filmrev/the_martix

45 Scarratt, ibid, 2001

46 Tasker, Spectacular Bodies: Gender, Genre and the Action Cinema, 1993

47 Scarratt, ibid, 2001

48 Dyer, Action! in Action/Spectacle Cinema, 2000

49 & 50 Street, ibid, 2001

51 The Matrix Revisited DVD, 2001

6. Institutions

Looking at the industrial landscape behind a contemporary Hollywood release is a fruitful exercise, particularly in relation to the cinematic 'event' movie. It is important to understand the economic as well as cultural background to contemporary media texts, not least because it goes a long way to explain the machinations of the dominant Hollywood film industry, as well as offering ways into studying audiences and cultural/generic patterns and tastes. However it is no longer sufficient merely to look at the film industry alone. Contemporary Hollywood is dominated by international conglomerates, whose interests cross the full spectrum of media and information platforms and who vertically and horizontally connect products and, therefore, meaning across the diverse companies they own. In the era of globalisation and new technology, it is conglomerates with interests spanning across a range of medias that have the 'edge', with convergence allowing for such companies to maximise profit and marketing potential.

One of the Hollywood film industry's biggest advantages is distribution on an international scale. **Distribution** is the acquisition of films from the production companies and the selling/renting of them to the **exhibition** circuit (cinemas). Here, it is argued, Hollywood can display elements of **vertical and horizontal integration**, the vertical ownership of each stage of a film's life – production, distribution and exhibition – and the horizontal ownership of multiple companies and media forms thus having control over the market place. This certainly applies with *The Matrix* and even more so with *Reloaded* (as discussed previously). The film was produced by Village Roadshow pictures, an Australian production company, alongside Silver Pictures (both potentially with option deals with the studio), and was distributed by Warner Bros., a part of the multimedia conglomerate AOL Time Warner. AOL Time Warner is a media giant, owning movie studios and production companies, cable TV and cartoon networks as well as TV production companies, AOL Internet Service Provider, music, book and magazine publishing companies, as well as, until recently, a cinema chain, making it perfectly placed to make the most of new technology and the digital world's rapidly changing market place.

With any film released, it will abide by a **release strategy**. This will be designed by the distributor, who will bear the costs of making the film prints – an expensive business, the number struck decided according to the film's potential appeal. The release strategy will also include the **marketing campaign**. It is important to remember that film budgets do not usually include marketing costs, which can be very significant. In crude terms, if a film is to do well in today's market, it will need money behind it – it isn't enough to make a film, it is how it appears in cinemas and finds its audience that will decide its box office fate. The *average* cost of marketing a $50m film has been put at $24.5m.[52] Films are consumer products. When an ad campaign tries to create a 'must see' factor, what they are doing is selling an unknown entity to the consumer as they will not have seen the film before. Many factors – time of year, target audience, genre – will play a part in the reception of a film. Hollywood operates on the assumption that most films will lose money, but that the hits will reap big rewards. Hence a continuous pattern of film releases tailored to different times of year – if enough are released and marketed properly, some will hit the jackpot. *The Matrix* was one of them.

The Matrix was released in the USA on 31 March 1999 (in the UK it was 11 June). It had a budget of $63 million – a large amount of money by many standards but in comparison to other films of the genre (sci fi/action), it was a 'middle budget' picture. Still, with *Bound* having cost a mere $5m, the leap upwards was a big one, possibly made easier by the pair being backed by long-time successful Hollywood producer Joel Silver (responsible for the *Lethal Weapon* series (1987–1998) as well as *Die Hard* (1988–1995)). Shooting the film in Australia significantly reduced the costs, allowing the film to be made to its budget (it also, allegedly, allowed for a freer creative reign due to being far away from the studio backers).

On its opening, *The Matrix* was released in 2849 cinemas across the US – this would be categorised as a **saturation** release (when large numbers of prints are made). Over its opening weekend in the US, the film took over $27m – then the biggest ever opening over an Easter weekend. It stayed at number one in the box office for two weeks and continued to steadily drop off at a slow rate over the following three months, giving it a long box office life and a considerably less harsh drop off than many releases. Of the total $456.4m the film made worldwide, $171m – less than half – was made at the US domestic box office. The film was an enormous hit in Britain and other parts of the world – vital in creating large returns. As was then standard practice, the film was

1999 WORLDWIDE BOX OFFICE TOP TEN

	Film	Budget	Distributor	Release Date (US)	Total Gross
1	Star Wars Episode I: The Phantom Menace	$115m	20th C. Fox	19 May 99	$923m
2	The Sixth Sense	$55m	BVI	8 June 99	$661.5m
3	Toy Story 2	$90m	Disney/BVI	24 Nov 99	$485.7m
4	**The Matrix**	$65m	Warner Bros.	31 March 99	$456.4m
5	Tarzan	$150m	Disney/BVI	18 June 99	$435.3m
6	The Mummy	$76m	UIP	5 July 99	$413.3m
7	Notting Hill	$42m	UIP	28 May 99	$363.1m
8	The World is Not Enough	$120m	UIP	19 Nov 99	$352.0m
9	American Beauty	$15m	UIP	17 Sept 99	$336.1m
10	Austin Powers:The Spy Who Shagged Me	$33m	Various	11 June 99	$310.3m

Source: http://www.boxofficereport.com

(NB: BVI is short for Buena Vista International – the same company as Disney but used for different types of film, UIP is short for United International Pictures)

released over two months earlier in the US than in the UK. As an industry practice this could allow distributors to save on print costs by shipping prints no longer needed in the US market overseas. Notable today is the narrower window of big film releases – *Reloaded* came out a mere seven days later in the UK. Much of this can be attributed to the threat to box office revenues of internet piracy, sometimes addressed by a simultaneous release worldwide (as happened with *Lord of the Rings: The Two Towers* in 2002).

Looking at the table above, the top ten box office hits of 1999 reveal much about the box office landscape the year *The*

Matrix was released.

First, a good comparison with *The Matrix* in terms of genre is *Star Wars Episode I: The Phantom Menace*. The film was science fiction, heavily reliant on special effects and arguably the most anticipated film for many years, being a follow on to a phenomenally successful prior trilogy. In a sense the film was a sequel and benefited from in-built multiple audience appeal – original fans and a huge potential new children's fanbase. Given its box office it did extremely well as one would expect, however companies investing heavily in *Phantom Menace* merchandising reported lesser profits than expected and, in some cases, losses.[53] Several of the other films were also sequels or part of franchises – *Toy Story 2*, *The World is Not Enough* (James Bond), *Austin Powers 2* – 'sure fire' hits. It is worth noting that sequels invariably cost more than the originals not least because of actor pay demands so you would expect them to have larger budgets, ad campaigns and high box office, at least initially. This is particularly true of the *Star Wars* films – the original, made in 1977, cost $10m compared to $115m for both *Phantom Menace* and *Attack of the Clones* (2002) and is similarly the case with the following two *Matrix* sequels (alleged to have a combined budget of over $250m).

Looking at the films in table, the majority are big budget, aimed at family or youth audiences or are star led (*Notting Hill*), but there are surprises, showing that despite everything the film industry tries to do, the public makes up its own mind. (It would be interesting to look at the 'failures' of the same year, for example *Wild Wild West* which made $217.8m but with a budget of $170m was considered a box office failure.) The 'sleeper' hits were *The Sixth Sense*, *American Beauty* and *The Matrix* – whilst *The Matrix* is a sci fi action film foregrounding special effects, its budget was only $10m more than *The Sixth Sense*. Similarly *The Mummy*, an action/adventure Indiana

Jones-style romp cost more than *The Matrix* and made less yet was still a considerable hit. Incidentally, comparing the budgets and special effects of the two films shows how much *The Matrix* was able to achieve for its money. Also, the majority of these films had family-friendly certification, helping them reach the widest possible audience. By contrast *The Matrix* was given an 'R' certificate in the US (whereby audience members under 17 are supposed to be accompanied by an adult) widely considered to be detrimental to box office performance. It was also released prior to the traditional time of year for the 'event' movie, usually reserved for late spring/ early summer to allow for long theatrical runs encompassing school holidays. Released in March over the Easter weekend, the film benefited from the holiday break business. However the film also opened before *The Phantom Menace* – a canny move that may have been able to capitalise on the anticipation for another science fiction film, and which may have positioned it well to pick up any adult audience fall-out from the largely child-centric *Phantom Menace*. The stunning visuals of *The Matrix* also lend it to multiple viewings, helping to sustain box office appeal over a longer period of time.

It would seem that the main surprise about *The Matrix* was not that it was a hit, but that it was such a big hit, out-performing films with twice the budget. But despite its apparent 'surprise' hit status, *The Matrix* – and nearly all the other films in the top ten for 1999 – was backed by a big studio distributor. The exception was *Austin Powers 2*, which was sold to different distributors in different 'territories' (countries). These international conglomerates can own a range of interests from communications networks to leisure complexes. This is an interesting point of study in itself. In relation to the top ten, it would mean that all of them had access to coherent international marketing and release strategies as well as potential add-on product tie-ins where appropriate. Warner Bros. was delighted that *The Matrix* established them as a more 'cutting edge' studio and at that point *The Matrix* was the highest grossing film the studio had produced.

As is custom now, there was a heavy promotion campaign when *The Matrix* was released on video and later on DVD. On both were 'making of' documentaries, a feature now reserved almost expressly for DVDs. At the time of its DVD release the format was still in its early stages of popularity and the film became the first DVD release to sell over a million copies. Lucrative TV/satellite deals would also have been made across the globe indicating further the importance of a successful post-cinema sales strategy for the distributor. Following on from *The Matrix* DVD a further DVD was released – *The Matrix Revisited*, offering over two hours of vignettes about the making of the film. DVD has been positioned as being able to offer far more than just the film, creating an expectation amongst buyers for something 'more'. This allows for a host of Special Editions, 'never before seen footage' and the like, further enhancing the longevity of a film's shelf-life (particularly one with technical prowess) as well as increasing engagement/interactivity between audience and text. A look at the accompanying anime shorts and games for *The Matrix Reloaded* further addresses this evolving cross-media fertilisation and audience immersion.

The Matrix Reloaded

Back in costume for The Matrix Reloaded

If in 1999 *The Matrix* was the antidote to the enormous hype anticipating the release of *The Phantom Menace*, 2003 saw the film's cult status elevate *The Matrix Reloaded* to those very proportions. Having overwhelmingly positive critical praise in addition to box office success and such cultural impact it inspired multiple insipid misappropriations, *The Matrix* was always going to be a tough act to follow.

Reloaded has several things in common with *Phantom Menace*. Critical response to the film has been relatively muted. Critics complained about the effects (not as impressive), the story (too self-important) and the film had an impossible task in living up to the first film's word of mouth appeal. Narratively, it also had to revisit an enigma that was, to all intents and purposes, 'solved' by the first film's conclusion. Much of the first film's hook was the 'what is *the matrix*?' element. Such a hook could never be repeated, even if the entire mystery were to be refuted and disproved. A film with so much hype inevitably comes with baggage and, like *Phantom Menace*, less than euphoric reviews did not stop people going to see the film. Dubbed by producer Joel Silver 'the Year of *The Matrix*', not only would 2003 produce one but two sequels, turning the original idea into a trilogy (which the

Wachowskis claim to have conceived prior to making the first one), and, undoubtedly, a **franchise**.

Let us look at the film text. The same main elements are all there – effects (this time going further and creating entirely CGI action shots featuring human figures), action sequences (notably impressive ones being the extended car chase and the Neo versus multiple Smiths fight), foregrounding of costume, iconography and further character and narrative development, in addition to the far more explicit philosophical referencing and a twist to arguably refute the conclusion of the first film. Zion is the most notable addition as a location, its majestic machinations styled on the drawings of Geoff Darrow, as well as the deliberately blank space of the Architect's abode. A multitude of new characters appear, some with recognisable functions, some making more sense after viewing *The Animatrix* (an interesting innovation on narrative – stretching it across multiple media forms more than any film has done previously). The names are derived from a mixture of mythologies – Persephone and Niobe from Greek mythology, the Japanese-inspired Merovingian, and in a literal play on words, the Keymaster. Noticeable also is the further emphasis on race. Zion is overwhelmingly black, a place where people of all colour and gender are given equal respect. Morpheus as leader of his people is given more time for characters other than Neo, and Trinity, by revealing her love at the end of the first film, has the hard act of maintaining female action-figure status while being in love with someone far more powerful not just than her but any human in the film. And Neo must face the responsibility that goes with power and the notions of choice and truth.

In terms of **box office**, as is common with such hyped releases, the film was proclaimed to have broken records in its opening weekend. Indeed it did – in the US alone it made

$91.8m in three days, the biggest opening of an R (restricted) rating film ever, and made $134.3m in its first four days – more than any other film in history.[54] In the UK the film was released on an enormous 919 prints, making £12.2m in its opening weekend, the largest 15-rated opening in the UK ever. Similarly in other key territories the world over the film's opening figures were staggering, leading to a worldwide take of $550m in the first four weeks,[55] already more than the entire theatrical run of the first film.

Hyperbole aside, the film was dethroned from the top spot in the US after only one week by the Jim Carrey comedy *Bruce Almighty*, which along with luke-warm reviews makes the success of *Reloaded* slightly more relative if measured by critical response, word of mouth and size of budget. Its long term total will no doubt continue to rise to vast proportion, but the differences between a mid-budget cult hit created by strong word of mouth (*The Matrix*) and a much-hyped, heavily-marketed, long anticipated blockbuster may only be fully visible post-cinematic release. *Reloaded* was, however, much more than a film or even a blockbuster – it was a media event, crossing a multitude of media forms and making it as innovative, albeit in a different way, as the first film.

Tying in with the style of the films bearing hallmarks of the computer game, with *Reloaded* came *Enter The Matrix*, for games consuls and web. Whilst a game tie-in is now fairly standard for big budget science fiction or fantasy films, the Wachowskis have changed the rules. Previously, characters or movie scenes were licensed, the game then created as a tie-in. With *Enter The Matrix*, the film's directors also directed and wrote the script for the game, including shooting an hour's extra footage with the film's actors involved. Instead of Neo being the hero, the game's focus is on two more minor characters in the film, Niobe and Ghost. Instead of the game being *based on* the film, the narrative of *Reloaded* is being told from different perspectives across as range of media platforms, making it the first true release of media convergence, creating an interface and re-mediation between gaming and cinema, where the meta-text offers different experiences of consumption across different platforms.

This is also demonstrated by *The Animatrix* which appeared very shortly after *Reloaded*'s cinema release. A DVD featuring nine computer animated shorts based on a range of animation techniques (predominantly Japanese *anime*, on which the Wachowskis claim to have based much of their storyboarding techniques), these shorts tell stories either of smaller characters or events featured in *Reloaded* (*Kid's Story* and *Final Flight of the Osiris*) or offering background history to the road towards the dominance of the machines (*The Second Renaissance Parts I & II*). The latter two in particular make uncomfortable viewing, with the cruel, destructive nature of the humans demonstrated through their treatment of the machines who are in turn humanised, clinging together in the face of violence, with imagery alluding to the Holocaust. As with Enter *The Matrix*, *Reloaded*'s narrative actually makes more sense after viewing *The Animatrix*. Whether this means the cross-overs – previously incidental in narrative terms (if not inconsiderable revenue earners) – render the trilogy's narrative progressive or actually are detrimental to it is an interesting area for debate.

These *animes* were also part of the build-up towards the film's release, several of them downloadable from the film's **website** at intervals in the months leading up to the film's release, along with trailers and a host of philosophical articles (highlighting the heavyweight themes backing up the visual splendour and popularising cultural and philosophical theory). *Final Flight of the Osiris* was released theatrically as a short film, accompanying *Dreamcatcher* (2003), a science fiction/ horror film from the same studio as *Reloaded*, Warner Bros. Not only was the short building anticipation for the sequels, it was also helping in the promotion of another film of a similar genre *and* selling a product in its own right, *The Animatrix* – a powerful demonstration of the marketing and earnings potential of a media conglomerate.

It should not – cannot – be overlooked that AOL Time Warner cover the range of media forms and, as discussed earlier, are fully able to take advantage of and create this type of multimedia release. So to what extent is *The Matrix Reloaded* a true release of convergence, a celebration and embracement of film as part of a wider series of (popular) media forms, and to what extent are they sophisticated marketing techniques? Of course they are inextricably linked, and as with all study of the media, there are no set rules, only theories. The element that categorically links them is *technology*. *The Animatrix* and *Enter The Matrix* may have been born of the fertile imaginations of the Wachowskis but they are, as with the films themselves, consumables.

52 King and Krzywinska, ibid, 2000

53 King and Krzywinska, ibid, 2000

54 Screen International, 30 May, 2003

55 www.screendaily.com

Filmography

The Matrix, DVD and VHS, Warner Bros., 1999

The Matrix Reloaded, DVD and VHS, Warner Bros., 2003

The Matrix Revisited, DVD, Warner Bros., 2001

Bibliography

Arroyo, J., 'The Big Loud Action Movie', in Arroyo, J. (ed.) *Action/Spectacle Cinema: A Sight and Sound Reader*, London: BFI, 2000

Bassham, G., 'The Religion of *The Matrix* and the Problems of Pluralism', in Irwin, W. (ed.) *The Matrix and Philosophy*, Chicago: Open Court, 2002

Brannigan, M., 'There is No Spoon: A Buddhist Mirror', in Irwin, W. (ed.) *The Matrix and Philosophy*, Chicago: Open Court, 2002

Dreyfus, H. and Dreyfus, S., 'The Brave New World of The Matrix', www.whatisthematrix.com

Dyer, R., 'Action!' in Arroyo, J. (ed.) *Action/Spectacle Cinema: A Sight and Sound Reader*, London: BFI, 2000

Erion, G. and Smith, B., 'Skepticism, Morality and *The Matrix*' in Irwin, W. (ed.) *The Matrix and Philosophy*, Chicago: Open Court, 2002

Hollows, J. and Jankovich, M., *Approaches to Popular Film*, Manchester: MUP, 1995

Jacobs, J., 'Gunfire', in Arroyo, J. (ed.) *Action/Spectacle Cinema: A Sight and Sound Reader*, London: BFI, 2000

King, G. and Krzywinska, T., *Science Fiction Cinema: From Outerspace to Cyberspace*, London: Wallflower, 2000

McDonald, P., 'Star Studies', in Hollows, J. and Jankovich, M., *Approaches to Popular Film*, Manchester: MUP, 1995

Neale, S., *Genre*, London: BFI, 1980

Neale, S., (ed.) *Genre and Contemporary Hollywood*, London: BFI, 2002

Newman, K., 'Rubber Reality' in *Science Fiction/Horror: A Sight and Sound Reader*, London: BFI, 2002

Rayner, P., Wall, P. and Kruger, S., *AS Media Studies: The Essential Introduction*, London: Routledge, 2001

Scarratt, E., *Science Fiction Film: A Teacher's Guide to the Genre*, Leighton Buzzard: Auteur, 2001

Storey, J., *An Introductory Guide to Cultural Theory and Popular Culture*, Hemel Hempstead: Harvester Wheatsheaf, 1993.

Street, S., *Costume and Cinema: Dress Codes in Popular Film*, London: Wallflower, 2001

Tasker, Y., *Spectacular Bodies: Gender, Genre and the Action Cinema*, London: Routledge, 1993

Tasker, Y., *Working Girls: Gender and Sexuality in Popular Cinema*, London: Routledge, 1998

Reviews/Articles

Smith, Adam, 'Reality Bites', *Empire*, July 1999

Conrad, Peter, 'Reloaded and Ready for Action', *The Observer Review*, 2 March 2003

Gordon, Devin, '*The Matrix* Makers', *Newsweek*, 6 January 2003

Romney, Jonathan, 'Everywhere and Nowhere' *Sight and Sound*, Vol 13, issue 7, 2003

And if you really want to 'Bake Your Noodle'...

Baudrillard, J. *Simulacra and Simulation*, Michigan: University of
Michigan Press, 1981

Websites

www.whatisthematrix.com
The official site for all three films offering a host of interviews with the
cast and crew, essays on the meaning of the films, trailers and stills.

www.enterthematrixgame.com
The official site of the game accompanying the release of *The Matrix
Reloaded*.

www.intothematrix.com
Again relating to *Reloaded*, this website showcases the anime shorts
released in June 2003 as *The Animatrix*.

www.the-movie-times.com/thrsdir/actors/kreeves
Website showing box office takings for Hollywood stars, including
Keanu Reeves.

www.imdb.com
The Internet Movie Database has a wealth of information on stars, box
office takings, tag lines... just about everything.

www.boxofficereport.com
Site offering worldwide box office statistics on films of recent years.

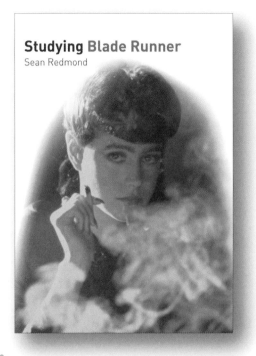

Studying Blade Runner
Sean Redmond

66 I found the range of information, depth of analysis and provocative arguments presented here quite eye-opening. 99

Media Education Jnl

"A complete scheme of work for the teaching and study of science fiction film."

Studying City of God

Stephanie Muir

"This is one of the best study guides I have seen... you would be foolish indeed to ignore this guide."

In the Picture

Studying Chungking Express
Sean Redmond

"Always interesting and extremely useful."
Media Education Jnl

NOTES

NOTES